FORGIVENESS

Michel Hubaut

FORGIVENESS

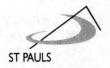

ST PAULS

Original title: *Pardonner oui ou non?*
© 1992 Desclée de Brouwer, Paris, France

Translated by Rachel Orbell

ST PAULS
Middlegreen, Slough SL3 6BT, United Kingdom
Moyglare Road, Maynooth, Co. Kildare, Ireland

English translation © ST PAULS (UK) 1994

ISBN 085439 475 3

Printed by Redwood, Trowbridge

ST PAULS is an activity of the priests and brothers of the Society of St Paul who proclaim the Gospel through the media of social communication

Contents

1.

"Oh, Sorry!" – A casual remark or a concept essential to humanity?

We say "sorry" or "excuse me" several times a day, when we bump into someone, when we are afraid of being a nuisance or when we interrupt in the course of a conversation. "Sorry" along with "yes", "no" and "thank you" are the first words of a foreign language to be learned, for the simple reason that they form the basis of all moral behaviour and of life in society. When we say we are sorry, we are putting ourselves second and showing respect for another person.

Although the word itself appears less often, 1992 has, strangely enough, seen a marked return to the theme of forgiveness, and this has happened well outside the sphere of religion. Television programmes, as well as newspaper articles and opinion polls have brought the subject to popular attention.

Does this perhaps herald a new awareness that, while hatred and violence continue to devastate certain parts of the world, forgiveness is essential if the human race is to survive?

Although private confession is on the decline, offi-

> In the following list of public gestures of forgiveness or acts of repentance, which do you find the most moving?*
>
> — *The Pope's forgiveness of his would-be assassin*   54%
>
> — *The parents who forgave the boy who shot their daughter because he was afraid she would leave him*   45%
>
> — *Lech Walesa's visit to Israel to ask forgiveness for Poland's stance during the war*   38%
>
> — *Willy Brandt, the German chancellor, kneeling at the memorial to the Warsaw ghetto*   30%
>
> — *José Canestro's forgiveness of his wife after her attempt to poison him*   28%
>
> — *Aldo Moro's daughter who forgave two members of the Italian Red brigade for the assassination of her father*   20%
>
> — *Don't know*   7%

cial gestures of forgiveness are nevertheless hitting the headlines. Few people could fail to be moved by pictures of Pope John Paul II visiting his would-be assassin in prison, of Willy Brandt kneeling before the memorial to the Warsaw ghetto, of the Czechoslovakian president Vaclav Havel who, in his first statement on foreign policy, asked forgiveness of the German Sudety minority for their expulsion from Czechoslovakia.

There have been striking pictures, too, of Juan Carlos, the king of Spain, apologising publicly in the

*The statistics given in this chapter are taken from an opinion poll published, in which questions were put to a representative sample of 800 people over the age of 18.

Madrid synagogue for the expulsion of the Jews in 1492.

According to the dictionary, to forgive means to regard an offence as never having been committed, and to refuse to exact vengeance. But there is a vast difference between someone treading on your toe and the murder of your child. Most people who have been physically or morally wounded or who have a loved one who has been a victim, will say – and often with vehemence – that there are some instances in which it is impossible, inhuman and certainly unnatural to forgive.

Is it ever impossible to forgive? In the cross-fire of interrogation, in the silence of grief, in cries of revolt, in replies cut short, in generous words or stammered responses, key questions arise which reach to the very heart of the human mystery, to the living out of life in society and to the very purpose of human existence itself.

In the following list of crimes or disasters, which ones would you, as a member of society, be unable to forgive?

– *The laundering of drug money*	*75%*
– *The taking of hostages*	*68%*
– *The infection of haemophiliacs*	*67%*
– *A racist attack*	*54%*
– *False accounting*	*44%*
– *Oil slicks*	*43%*
– *Desertion in time of war*	*26%*
– *Don't know*	*1%*

Why should one forgive? How often should forgiveness be offered? Are there such things as "unforgivable" crimes? Can one forgive without condoning the crime? How can forgiveness and justice be reconciled?

Can those who have been deeply wounded completely free themselves of all feelings of hatred and vengeance? Can one forgive a person who shows no remorse for what they have done? Can one forgive on the victim's behalf?

Individually or collectively can we, or should we, "forget"? Does forgiveness result from cowardice or from selflessness? Could forgiveness simply be seen as a way of disguising our inability to resolve conflicts and end injustice? Can human beings achieve any kind of inner peace in their lives or can a future be built without forgiveness? Can society survive without reconciliation?

In your opinion, forgiveness is:	
— *Love for one's neighbour*	*51%*
— *A necessity in society*	*35%*
— *A moral obligation*	*34%*
— *An act of faith*	*26%*
— *A sign of weakness*	*11%*
— *A denial of justice*	*9%*
— *Don't know*	*4%*

Is it possible for human beings to forgive? Or is not forgiveness an ultimate ideal towards which we can strive, but to which we can never fully attain? Does the Judeo-Christian revelation have any new light to shed on the subject? Is there a specifically "Christian" forgiveness?

10

These are all questions with which we shall attempt to deal in the chapters which follow, without claiming to provide any definite answers. Each individual will be able to find a starting point for reflection which will help them to look more clearly into their own conscience and their own behaviour.

In the following list of wrong-doers, whom would you be unable to forgive?

- *Someone who is HIV positive who infects you with AIDS* — 57%
- *The hooligan who threatens you in the street* — 50%
- *The doctor who makes an error in your treatment* — 42%
- *The friend who goes off with you partner* — 36%
- *The driver who injures one of your family* — 32%
- *The partner who is unfaithful to you* — 28%
- *The hooligan who takes your car* — 26%
- *The manager who gives you the sack* — 18%
- *Don't know* — 4%

2.

When forgiveness seems impossible...

Forgiveness is a difficult and sensitive subject, since each person approaches it from their own experience, with their own memories and their own wounds. One individual (or group of people) may perceive it as a threat, as mere hypocrisy, as an unjustifiable act of cowardice or, alternatively, as an attitude essential to the safeguarding of their identity and their future.

In June 1942, Simon Wiesenthal was called to the deathbed of a young SS officer who wanted to ask forgiveness of a Jew before he could die in peace. Wiesenthal refused to allow him this peace.

"As soon as I left him, I was obsessed by this incident. And I still am. In the end, my whole life has revolved around this refusal. Was I right or wrong to withhold forgiveness? ... I cannot explain why I behaved as I did, since I believe he was genuinely sorry.

"But there was still the grief and the suffering which I endured, and which I saw so many others endure. What would have given me the right to forgive on behalf of those whom I had watched die?"

> *Forgiveness! But have they ever asked for our forgiveness? Only the wretchedness and distress of the criminal would make forgiveness reasonable and relevant. When the criminal is well-fed and well-off and has prospered under the economic miracle, forgiveness is a cruel joke. Forgiveness died in the death camps.*
>
> Vladimir Jankélévitch, talking about Nazi war criminals

In her book *The Rape of Silence* Eva Thomas, who was raped by her father at the age of fifteen, tells how it took her over thirty years to overcome the sense of her own guilt and voice her anger. By speaking out, she freed herself from the shame which had burdened her and which had kept her hatred in check.

But she has no time for forgiveness. Brought up as a Catholic, she detests the very word. "Christian forgiveness, which demands that one should regard a crime as non-existent, is nothing short of hypocrisy. As for the synonyms suggested in the dictionary such as 'mercy', 'absolution', 'indulgence', 'grace' ... such attitudes are impossible for a victim of incest."

The media has brought to light many true stories illustrating a range of attitudes and experiences. There is, for example, the couple whose only child, a boy of three, was abused and killed, who ask: "How do you expect a parent to forgive the murderer of their child?"

"I am not someone who finds it easy to forgive and I do not want to forgive, because if I let go of my hatred and bitterness, I lose a little of my ground in my battle against incest", explains a woman who was raped by her father at the age of twelve, and who has taken him to court.

Then there is the story of a man whose family died at the hands of Paul Touvier during the war. He himself only survived by a miracle, and he asks: "Must I forgive this criminal who refuses to acknowledge his crimes?" There is no answer to such a question except silence, a sacred, inviolable, depthless silence, the silence of the memory of Shoah, of the extermination of the Jews, the silence of God.

In the strict sense of the term, there is only a fine line between forgiveness and insanity, and the same can be true of remorse, sacrifice and the impulse towards charity.

Vladimir Jankélévitch

Liberation from hatred and the renewal of the human soul

There are others who, without claiming any particular religious motivation, succeed in overcoming the difficulties and offering forgiveness out of a kind of faith in love and in the future of humanity. Witness the singer who, on the night that his wife was brutally murdered, wrote to his friends:

"It is society itself which is sick. It is up to us to set it to rights through love, friendship and persuasion. That is what she lived for, my dearest love whose life has ended in her thirty-second year. We must not lose heart, neither you nor I. My life will go on; I will journey on with this extra burden to bear and with my two dear children to remind me of her.

"I cannot tell you what to do, but I would just ask you to love more than ever those who are nearest to you. The world is so sad and cheerless. The pure in heart must unite. To bring colour to the world, the human soul must blossom and flower. I will remain a gardener, I will tend my plants, the words which I sing.

"Through the words I use you will recognise my beloved. Nothing is true but friendship and love. For the moment I have sunk very low in the morass of sadness... So now, in the face of what has happened to me, I am taking the liberty of writing to you, my friends, I, who am no more than an actor, a player, an entertainer building castles in the air; I am taking the liberty of telling you my thoughts: I believe with all my heart that we must love one another whatever happens."

We must acknowledge and respect such a diversity of feelings and reactions amongst the victims of evil and we must recognise how difficult it is to forgive. We should not be shocked by the fact that it is the desire for vengeance which arises spontaneously in the human heart.

Excessive suffering, a fear of rendering horror commonplace and condoning wrong-doing, a confusion between forgetting and forgiving, the compelling need to see that justice is done; these can all be obstacles to forgiveness. There are even some who regard forgiveness as being beneath human dignity.

"Christian forgiveness", when seen as a sentimental and hypocritical exercise, sometimes provokes an instinctive feeling of revulsion which calls into question the way in which it is presented and lived out by the community of the faithful.

Reconciliation and forgiveness are gaining ground in the life of international relations. In the late twentieth century, they are the most subversive ideas which humanity has discovered in its quest for survival.

François Scholosser

Yet while we can understand the reaction of Jankélévitch and his claim that "Forgiveness died in the death camps", it is not a response which we can accept. Surely that is the whole point of forgiveness: to forgive the unforgivable. It is as gratuitous as love.

And while we must respect the attitude of each individual – for what would we do in their place? – we cannot ignore the fact that forgiveness is an integral part of the biblical and Christian revelation. But what does this forgiveness involve?

3.

Neither indebted nor forgetful

We do, nevertheless, sometimes hear of gestures which suddenly redefine the limits of our humanity, leaving us speechless with admiration or amazement as we see the impossible lived out or catch a glimpse of transcendence.

One survivor of the 1986 bomb blast in Paris in which seven people died and fifty-five were injured, still manages to smile, in spite of now having to walk with a stick. During the subsequent trial she made no pretence of her Christian faith, a faith which left her actively interested in the outcome, but not vindictive.

She gives her testimony modestly out of respect for the other victims. Without ostentation she says quite simply that she forgives. She was prepared to say so publicly in the witness box if the accused showed any sign of remorse. They are loving words which she is already living out, words spoken in her own name, not in the name of the organisation "SOS Bomb Attack" of which she is an active member.

"Forgiveness is an individual not a collective step. At the last judgement, I will answer for my own actions,

> *My response to this series of crises was one of blindness, anger, deceit, resignation and finally forgiveness. No one asked anything of me. All I know is that I can now live without bitterness, without being consumed by hatred. I am not giving in, rather I have gained a new understanding, a new way of looking at things.*
>
> Tracy Chamoun

and so will the person who carried out the attack. We will not be required to answer for the actions of our predecessors nor for our contemporaries."

She sees forgiveness primarily as something silent. "It involves freeing one's heart from the poison of hatred. Life becomes mere slavery if one has no love for others and no humanity. Forgiveness means reconciliation, freedom and a greater degree of openness to the world."

In the previous chapter we described instances of dreadful suffering in which any gesture of human forgiveness seemed impossible. Beside these experiences we can set some Christian testimonies which unexpectedly break through the barriers of suffering and unforgiveness. Tracy Chamoun, the daughter of an assassinated Maronite Christian leader, explains with moving simplicity how, in spite of the horrors of the war, her Christian faith enabled her to discover a way to forgiveness. She describes her human and spiritual journey in her book *In the Name of the Father*:

"It was in 1988. I could no longer distinguish between truth and falsehood. I was torn apart. I was nearing thirty and my eyes were opened...

"For myself, I believe that I had to go through all these trials in order to become aware of my faith ... to cleanse myself, to carry out a task of self-discovery."

Maria Fida Moro, whose father was brutally murdered by the Italian Red Brigade in 1978, not only forgave the terrorists, but had a Mass of reconciliation celebrated in their prison.

Her gesture provoked sarcasm and hostility even in Catholic Italy. Her response to those who accused her of forgetting the two hundred dead, the blood and the unheeded tears, was this:

"One can never forget. I will never forget the sight of my father's body bundled into the boot of a red Renault. But one can forgive. I believe that this life is only a journey and that our true destiny as human beings lies elsewhere. I am striving for a new humanity, with no hatred and no vengeance. Forgiveness is something personal, private, intimate; it is a matter for the individual conscience. When I forgive, I perform a Christian gesture. It is a gesture which, in my place, my father would not have failed to make."

Forgiveness is the noblest form of solidarity.

Amine Gemayel,
former president of the Lebanese Republic

Faith can transcend the limits of humanity

"Forgiveness: neither indebtedness nor forgetfulness" is the title of a television documentary produced in Quebec which retraced the story of a horrifying incident. In 1979, two youngsters from Montréal were murdered and thrown into the St Lawrence River. The murderers arrested were two twenty-five year-olds.

The families reacted differently: one father, who

claimed to have no religion, chose to live and forget – which he tried to do in the peace of his garden – rather than to forgive.

But the parents and sister of the other victim drew on their Christian faith to find the strength to forgive. They even wrote to one of the murderers in prison, who told how he found this a "crazy" gesture, adding: "The letter was full of nothing but love."

They also wrote to his family, drawing them, too, along their own path of irrational love which ended at last in their meeting ten years after the incident had taken place.

Words fail at the sight of this couple walking calmly into the prison hand in hand, and greeting their daughter's murderer as if they were hugging a little child. There are no words adequate to express the overwhelming emotion of that moment. One is jolted onto another plane by a nobility and generosity which transcend humanity.

There have been other examples of such extraordinary gestures; in October 1982, a young man killed his girl friend because he thought she loved him less than he loved her. During the trial in 1984, the girl's parents declared publicly that they had forgiven him. "We received a letter from him asking for our forgiveness." They too wished to meet the murderer's family and share the traumatic experience with them.

"He is the one who needs our help", they explained. "We have come to regard him as our adopted child." And they too confide that the secret source of their strength is their Christian faith.

4.
Forgiveness requires more than human strength

In the end, I believe that forgiveness is not something we are capable of in our own strength. The following true story is an illustration of what I mean.

During the interminable conflict in the Lebanon, I was the guest of several Christian communities who invited me to share their fears and their hopes in the face of a tragedy to which no one could see any solution.

Beirut was divided. One could hear cannons rumbling away somewhere above the town. Snipers, concealed in gutted buildings or at street corners, shot systematically at anyone, men or women, who came into their line of fire.

One evening, near the Church of Our Lady of Harissa which overlooks the majestic bay of Jouniah, I was with a group of Lebanese friends who had invited round several of their neighbours. One of the men present suggested we should read a chapter of the Gospel to bring to a close the fellowship we had shared. Opening his book, he found the passage set for that day in the liturgy. After a brief hesitation, he glanced round the expectant group, and then began to read:

"Peter approached Jesus and said to him: Lord, how many times must I forgive my brother if he sins against me? As many as seven times? Jesus replied to him: I tell you not only seven times but seventy times seven!"

A long and painful silence followed. These were men and women scarred by long years of a war in which they had all lost at least one member of their family. The little that I had learned of their suffering made me understand instinctively the enormity of what had been read. The Gospel passage suddenly seemed inhuman.

These people were trapped in suffering by a situation which they had not brought about and which they were powerless to change. How could one preach such a message to them? As they overcame the pain they felt, they gained the courage to talk. And I listened in awe as they humbly acknowledged, in voices broken by suffering, that forgiveness does not come naturally to hearts that have been crushed by so much hatred, blood and death.

Following this honest confession they began to pray spontaneously. They asked God to create in them, through the power of the Spirit, this impossible capacity for forgiveness. The sincerity and generosity of their prayer made a deep impression. When the meeting ended late at night, one of them drove me home. As we said good-bye, he offered me some money: "Father, please will you say a Mass for my two sons, a seventeen year-old and a twenty year-old, both of them dead..." He paused and then added: "They were tortured. They had their eyes and tongues torn out."

I felt stunned by this atrocity, and before I could react he handed me more money, saying: "And please say another Mass for those who killed them." I could not reply. All I could do was shake his hand in the long silence.

As I went to bed that night, I found that my heart was full of thanksgiving in spite of the horror of all that I had heard. How great, Lord, is one who is wounded yet able to forgive! I suddenly realized that forgiveness can be one of the most beautiful manifestations of the Spirit in the human heart.

The gesture this man had made required a strength far greater than his own. That night I understood that to forgive is truly to share in the gift of God, to participate in the graciousness of his infinite love. To think in human terms is to be trapped in a spiral of hatred, of vengeance which generates vengeance and evil which breeds evil. But this spiral is decisively, illogically and irrationally broken by the gift of forgiveness.

What might have seemed weakness or capitulation suddenly becomes a radical step, an unexpected movement of the Spirit. What an amazing leap, to go from human logic, to the logic of God, the logic of love which died once on Calvary crying out: "Forgive them."

When faced with people such as this who are indwelt by the Holy Spirit, the petty offences which we, in our pride, elevate into points of honour, seem pitiful and trifling. The forgiveness offered by this Lebanese Christian was, I believe, deeply rooted in the heart of God. Thanks to him, I was able to see how faith could bring an end to the cycle of death. I went to sleep with the thought that while ever people of this calibre exist, in spite of the killings and the most barbaric kinds of slaughter, the earth will not be completely devoid of hope.

The following is an extract from a book written by a woman, Francine Cockenpot, who was savagely attacked in her own home. For a long time afterwards she struggled with her own feelings before she was finally able to forgive.

It is hard for me to forgive you for what you did to me...
It is not in my power to forgive you.
Ask forgiveness of Him who created the beasts as well as human beings.
Ask forgiveness of Him who knows that you are not a beast but a human being...
I no longer have it in me to think like this, for the very thing you have wounded in me is the image of humanity.
Ask Him and forget me, I stand in your way...
From You I await the experience of forgiveness.
Not a forgiveness which turns away, not one which forgets, but one which remembers in order to love more deeply, and to give new life to that which was lifeless.
From You, I await the strength to see my attacker as a brother whom I did not know soon enough to prevent, through my love, from becoming a murderer...
Farewell.
Go on living your life. I will try to go on living mine.
They will never be the same, neither your life nor mine...
Between you and me stands a life which has been ruined, and perhaps some hope...
of another life of which I know nothing, of which you know nothing.
Another life, another land whose earth has been nourished by blood and fire.
Another life for me and for you.
Perhaps, Lord...
When I stand before You,
I will speak first of all about him.
Perhaps no one else will ever have talked to You about him.

Perhaps no one else will ever have asked You so insistently that he be Your prodigal son...

Can You forgive me for saying: "Do not save me without saving him."

Father, into Your hands I commend his soul.

Take it, bleeding and tortured, and return it to him, at peace.

Human justice gives no peace,

but either condemns to remorse or incites to revenge...

You alone make us stand upright.

You alone, with a look of love, transform into human beings those who were living as beasts.

I did not know that You were going to allow his salvation to be linked to mine by bloodshed.

Father, into Your hands I commend our souls.

5.
Forgiveness does not mean making excuses

Before we go on to try and discover what constitutes forgiveness in the gospels, it would be useful to clear up some common misconceptions and to establish what forgiveness is not.

"One must try to put oneself in the other's place in order to understand and forgive." But does a purely intellectual understanding of the offender's past, their psychology and the attenuating circumstances behind their actions, enable us to forgive? It may allow us to make excuses for them but this is not the same as forgiveness. Forgiveness is gratuitous and does not necessarily require us first to understand.

If we make excuses, we risk seeing the offender as irresponsible and their actions as less than criminal. If we lessen the seriousness of the offence by excusing it, are we not denying the offender's responsibility and freedom, even their very existence? If there is to be forgiveness, there must be a fault to forgive.

If we act as if nothing has happened in the lives of the two people involved, are we not trying to turn back the clock? Such a situation merely renders any personal encounter impossible.

> *Supposing one punished an executioner by inflicting on him the same kind of suffering which he had inflicted on others... that one torturer would not have a hundred bodies in which to suffer the hundred martyrdoms for which he has been responsible. The punishment would not go far enough. It would remain incomplete and would only prove its powerlessness in the face of the crime.*
>
> France Quéré speaking at a conference on torture,
> Basle, 1990

There is no denying that both the offender and the victim need time. They will often experience a loss of any sense of self and be incapable of recognising each other immediately after a crime, especially a serious one. Time teaches patience, providing an opportunity for a slow process of cleansing and allowing space in which to prepare for a fresh encounter.

> *Forgiveness exists for this very reason: to forgive what no excuses can excuse. For there is no offence so serious that it cannot ultimately be forgiven... If there are crimes so monstrous that the perpetrator can never atone for them, we can still have recourse to forgiveness, since forgiveness is there precisely for hopeless or impossible cases.*
>
> Vladimir Jankélévitch

But to assume that "time will heal" is to deny the possibility of forgiveness. Time dissipates forgiveness without creating the possibility of a new future. The same thing applies on a collective level. One can analyse the various social, economic and psychological factors which gave rise to Nazism, but this kind of in-depth understanding does not necessarily imply an attitude of forgiveness for its atrocities.

Gospel forgiveness, as seen in the life and teaching of Christ, involves far more than a sympathetic understanding of the wretchedness of the human condition.

Even without any particular belief, human beings are capable of living out something which resembles forgiveness. They are generally more ready to talk in terms of "pity" for the human condition.

Schopenhauer and Camus recognise that freedom is conditioned by an awareness of its limitations. Perhaps there is a kind of forgiveness implicit in this feeling of pity for humanity and the wretchedness of human existence? But for all its generosity and magnanimity, this egalitarian attitude still falls short of the kind of forgiveness we encounter in the gospels.

Another possible caricature of true forgiveness is the suggestion that it arises out of fear and a need for security and that it is offered merely in order to escape from conflict. But forgiveness can never be achieved at the expense of responsibility, nor can it be prompted by fear, since this would provide no basis for the building of a new future.

6.

"Forgive, but do not forget"

At the entrance to the crypt of the memorial to the deportation in Paris are the words "Forgive. Do not forget."

Very often, when someone says that they will never forgive, they are really saying that they will never forget.

Indeed, the failure to distinguish between forgiving and forgetting is one of the most common mistakes to be made. Forgiving is not the same as forgetting, and just because we have forgotten it does not mean that we have forgiven. It is not simply a question of wiping the slate clean or of turning the page as if nothing has happened.

While forgiveness enables the offender to regain a sense of their own dignity, it can never be at the price of forgetting. As the psalmist says: "My fault is ever before me." Forgiveness does not involve forgetting, but rather owning the past in order to change it.

There are those who prefer to have nothing to do with a person who has committed an offence against them. They want to forget, to allow time to do its work; but they have not forgiven. One does not need to be a trained psycho-analyst to know that so-called forgotten wounds leave behind all sorts of ineradicable physical, mental and spiritual scars. Forgetting may suppress anger and stifle the desire for vengeance, but it can never wipe away the past.

> *There can be no forgiveness without an admission of guilt... We must explore what lies behind our silence. Our society must be willing to search out the truth about itself. We must face the unbearable and, together, learn from the past.*
>
> Cardinal Decourtray, speaking about the annihilation of the Jews at the hands of the Nazis

If we are to forget, we must necessarily refuse all contact with the offender in order to eliminate them completely from our memory. But is it possible to forgive an offence which one has effaced from one's mind? There is nothing worse than silence, and where a dialogue between offender and victim proves impossible, the victim often needs, even if only at the trial itself, to see and recognise the offender, to try and discover some sign of remorse in their expression or in their words.

To forgive without remembering is unworthy of humanity, since memory is an integral part of our being human. It is to its shame that France was unwilling to listen to the survivors of the death camps in 1945, and that during the trial of Pétain, there was not a single mention of Shoah.

In a television programme, Simone Veil spoke of her return from the hell she had experienced: "I wanted to talk, to say where I had been and what I had lived through, but no one would listen to me, no one wanted to know. And then we were blamed for our silence."

> *Are your sins so precious that they must be listed, classed and recorded in order on tablets of stone ... so that you can weigh them up and reproach yourself for them and commemorate them with great piety?*
>
> Péguy

It is not enough to feel angry about Touvier and to "forget" that France, by keeping silent, condoned the treatment of the Jews, the yellow stars, the round-up of Vel d'Hiv, the camps at Pithviers, Drancy, the departures for Auschwitz...

Christian forgiveness does not call for the eradication of memories. Instead, the Church must always remember what human beings were capable of during the war, and the extent of their cowardice. Presenting the report on Touvier to his priests, Cardinal Decourtray said:

"The granting of forgiveness in the name of Christ, that very forgiveness which we can experience in the sacrament of confession, presupposes certain conditions which are essential if it is to be given and received in a valid way: confession, repentance, reparation. The sacrament of forgiveness has never been seen as an attempt to invalidate human justice. The role which has been given to us to exercise in the name of God is not an alternative to the responsibility of society."

Does memory foster vengeance?

Clearly we must respect the distinction between forgiving and forgetting. But what kind of memory should we retain? An obsessional, bitter memory can be unhealthy and become nothing less than inner torture.

In this case, Nietzsche's comment is pertinent: "There

35

can be no happiness, no serenity, no hope, no pride, no enjoyment of the present, without the ability to forget."

Memories become intolerable if they are merely feeding a desire for vengeance. In the eighteenth century, the traditional practice of a "vendetta" led to the death of two-thirds of the Corsican population.

Corsica refused to forget. It was a kind of duty to keep a record of all the wrongs done to one's family, all the crimes committed against them in years long past. After several generations, hearts were as heavily burdened as memories.

Memories were retained simply for the sake of vengeance; a solemn, ritualised vengeance, viewed as a kind of pious duty towards the dead. Vengeance became a never-ending cycle, trapping the whole family in a spiral of death.

> *Careless people simply put their worries and cares aside. They shrug off offences and bitterness... But sadly, putting aside, shrugging off and turning the page are not the way to relate to others; they are ways of putting an end to all communication. The other person is thrown overboard along with one's cares and one's old nightmares... Finding a way to "be rid off" is not a moral problem.*
>
> Vladimir Jankélévitch

"If you remember that your neighbour has something against you..."

In Christian tradition forgiving and forgetting are kept very separate but, in addition, a central place is given to the act of remembrance. On the night before he died, Jesus said to his disciples: "Do this in memory of me." How should we then advocate forgetting?

Jesus himself established a link between memory and the consciousness of wrong-doing: "When you go to present your offering at the altar, if you remember that your neighbour has something against you, leave your offering where it is and go first and be reconciled to them." In order to be forgiven, we must remember what we have done wrong and accept responsibility for our own actions.

But this kind of remembrance should not promote either the desire for vengeance, or morbid guilt. As Péguy said, we should not keep rehearsing past faults. We must remember our past, not for our own satisfaction, in order to keep hold of our bitterness and resentment, but so that we can be alive to the present moment and committed to the future.

7.

Forgiveness
is the perfection of justice

"It's not fair!" may be the words of a child, but they illustrate how hard it is for human beings to put up with what they regard as injustice. Forgiveness can never make light of the demands of justice. An act of forgiveness is not a substitute for laws nor for the judges who must decide on the offender's guilt and a suitable punishment.

In human and social relationships there can be no separation between justice and mercy, two concepts which biblical tradition has always linked. For Christ himself, forgiveness never implied leniency or compromise with the evil in humanity which he unhesitatingly brought to light and denounced.

Yet he never identified the sinner with their sin. Respect for a person does not mean closing one's eyes to their fault, but doing everything possible to liberate them from it and to let them know that they are of greater value than the evil which devours them.

In Christian tradition there is never any conflict between justice and charity since forgiveness is directed at the person and not the evil they have done. A wrongdoing remains wrong and, as such, deserves punishment.

> *We learn from the past and from our own experience that justice is insufficient in itself and can even lead to its own negation and destruction, unless love, in all its depth and strength, is brought to bear in every aspect of human life.*
>
> Pope John Paul II, *Rich in mercy*

The aim of punishment should be the liberation of the offender

It is essential that punishment should not be experienced as a kind of legalised, public exaction of vengeance; but this is often how it appears. The principle of punishment and reparation is necessary in order to prevent the accused from being trapped within their guilt.

What of the demand that a person should "pay for what they have done"? It is very often the case that an offender is, in fact, incapable of making a full reparation for the far reaching consequences of the wrong they have committed. And besides, the duty to "pay" for what they have done by being punished ought never to be seen in terms of vengeance demanded by society, but rather as a path which will lead them towards a rehabilitation in their own eyes.

Any "punishment" should be aimed at helping the offender to rediscover their own value as a responsible human being and at the same time, showing them that human beings can never be completely identified with the wrong they have done. Such an attitude allows society to punish, the victim to forgive and the offender to ask forgiveness.

> *True mercy is the most profound form of justice. If justice in itself is the right means of "judging" between people in order to share out material things with fairness, love, in contrast, and love alone (and thus that loving kindness which we call mercy) is able to give human beings a sense of their own self. Truly Christian mercy is, in a certain sense, the most perfect manifestation of equality between human beings and thus too, the most perfect manifestation of justice...*
>
> Pope John Paul II, *Rich in mercy*

Mercy reaches further than justice

It is none the less true that there are times when we are torn between the logic of love and a moral obligation to put a stop to violence and to protect society from being destroyed by the evil which pervades it.

How can we reconcile these two demands in our conscience? There is no easy way to balance forgiveness against the punishment imposed by justice. In the encyclical, *Rich in mercy* – in which the close connection between mercy and justice is one of the issues addressed repeatedly – Pope John Paul II writes: "The new and legitimate sensitivity of contemporary society concerning the whole question of justice, risks, at times, to discredit any feeling of mercy which is seen as nothing more than a guilty indifference towards oppression and a lack of solidarity in the struggle against injustice."

In the Pope's view, the kind of mercy in which forgiveness is an essential element brings a new emphasis and a new content to the idea of justice which becomes something more than a mere punishment or the exaction of a payment. According to the Pope, mercy is the highest form of justice.

Quoting the old saying "Summum jus, summa injuria", he points out that history is full of examples illustrating how, by taking human justice to its logical conclusion, it can be perverted into the highest form of injustice.

"This statement does not detract from the value of justice... It simply highlights the necessity for a reliance on even deeper spiritual strengths, which affect the very ordering of justice itself" (No. 2).

While human justice is able to arbitrate, punish, or establish a fair sharing of material possessions, only merciful love is able to restore to human beings a sense of their own worth, for human beings have as much need of love as of justice. Mercy alone allows for justice without vengeance, without the humiliation of the other person, and makes possible a forgiveness which involves neither cowardice nor compromise.

The Pope reminds us that the source of all true justice is the loving mercy of God, which transcends our human definitions.

> *Love is the condition of justice and in the end, justice is the servant of charity. The primacy and superiority of charity over justice (which is apparent throughout the revelation) is revealed precisely in mercy.*
>
> Pope John Paul II, *Rich in mercy*

Giving and forgiving

There is no doubt that for followers of Christ, forgiveness goes further than strictly human justice, and flows from the boundless generosity of God.

Giving and forgiving are connected not only through

their etymology, but also by their content. Both are concerned with a freely willed exchange. To give is not simply to lend. To forgive is not simply to let someone off a debt. Giving and forgiving transcend the order of so-called "distributive" justice. One does not give because one owes something, one does not forgive by constraint. Giving and forgiving belong to the order of the "heart", in the sense in which that word is used by Pascal and in the Bible. We have gone beyond the simple rationality of human relationships. We sense that forgiveness is the will to live anew, the desire to start again and learn afresh.

Why should it be the victim who makes the first move?

Strangely enough it is often the victim who has to make the first move and forgive the one who has hurt them. Why should this be?

Christ's own actions shed particular light on this very human situation. The wrong which the offender has done affects that person as much as their victim; those who commit an offence degrade and even destroy themselves. They are disfigured in their own eyes and stand greatly in need of rehabilitation. They need to have their sense of their own dignity restored.

Which of the two suffers the greater hurt? If the victim's suffering is the greater subjectively, it is often the wrong-doer who is damaged more deeply in their humanity.

Mercy alone, such as that manifested by Christ, is capable of creating justice without humiliating the other person, allowing forgiveness to be accepted without any surrender to evil. Mercy gives us the strength to discover a kind of justice which does not crush human beings, which liberates rather than condemns. In Jesus alone, love and truth are united.

Human dignity as the purpose of mercy is perhaps the most constant theme in all of John Paul II's teaching. It is found in every one of his addresses. "We may at times be aware of an inequality, especially where mercy is concerned, between the one who offers it and the one who receives. As a result we may conclude that mercy offends the one who is its object and so offends human dignity" (No. 6).

But mercy bears the face of love; it is the deep and life-giving force which reveals to human beings their own true identity. It is the source of their humanity. Both those who forgive and those who are forgiven prove that human greatness lies in the rediscovery and recovery of human dignity.

8.

Is there such a thing as absolute and unforgivable evil?

Running throughout Judeo-Christian tradition we find two firmly held beliefs; firstly, that every sinful action is primarily an offence against the love of God who does not will evil, and secondly that, since no human being is innocent, no one can presume to throw the first stone.

If, however, we argue that we are all sinners and members together of a kind of communion of evil, we run the risk of trivialising evil and denying the need for a system of ethics to govern human beings and life in society. If all human beings are merely victims of evil, are there no torturers? And why bother to remember if no one is responsible?

Forgiveness presupposes that people accept responsibility for their actions and are able to repent. The discovery of the Nazi concentration camps made this point all the more significant.

The genocide carried out by the Nazis – similar in some ways to forms of genocide perpetrated against the American Indians or African slaves – has forced us into a new kind of awareness. With victory in the war came

> *Without the confession of the sinner, sin is swallowed up in the swirling mists of history. Without forgiveness for the one who repents, violence answers violence and sin is reinforced.*
>
> Jean Daniel

an obligation to acknowledge the existence of one specific crime within the hierarchy of evil, an absolute evil which could not be tolerated by humanity. A "crime against humanity" had been committed which was decreed unpardonable by law.

As a general principle a person would not expect to be held responsible under the law for the actions of their nation, family or other grouping, nor for an offence committed by themselves in a given past. This indicates a recognition that justice can evolve and that the human personality can change after a certain amount of time.

However, it was decided that the "Nazi evil" could not be made relative by time but would always remain a punishable offence. Should forgiveness be denied to these criminals once and for all? Would it not be possible to envisage the possibility of forgiveness, after a great deal of time, for those who recognise their guilt and repent?

Those who repent sincerely, freely, publicly and without reservation, contribute in their own way to the exposure of evil. By acknowledging their own guilt they renounce that evil. By repentance they accept the necessity of a scale of values and recognise society's code of ethics.

Finally, repentance is the only possible criterion by which a distinction can be made between forgiveness and complicity with evil. When a person repents they own the wrong they have done and accept responsibility for their actions. They need no longer be identified with their crime in the eyes of others, whose forgiveness opens up the possibility of a future.

The Churches in Eastern Europe, as in Czechoslovakia for example, which have been brave enough to ask forgiveness for the serious compromises made by certain clerics and members of their hierarchy with those in power during the totalitarian regimes, understood that their congregations needed such an act of repentance, made in public, so as to be able to go forward together into the future.

Should we forgive those who do not ask forgiveness?

Is it possible to forgive those who do not show the least sign of remorse, who do not acknowledge their guilt, and who even refuse or scorn forgiveness when it is offered by the person they have wronged? Is forgiveness inseparable from confession and repentance? We must be prepared to listen to a whole range of opinions in response to such questions. How can true forgiveness be offered to strangers or to those who have not asked forgiveness? – a situation which is common among families who have lost loved ones in a bomb blast or through crime.

There is no doubt that forgiveness can only be a liberating experience for the offender if they themselves have asked for and received that forgiveness. It requires a look, a gesture, an exchange of words: "Peter, do you love me?"

This is why victims of violence, or their relatives, may often be impatient to attend a trial and be confronted by the criminal; such a confrontation can lead to a completely new situation. There are those who even go as far as daring to visit the offender in prison, in the hope of hearing an appeal for forgiveness.

Such a gesture is liberating for all concerned. Several prison warders have told me that very often one of the greatest causes of suffering among prisoners is the absence of even the slightest glimmer of forgiveness.

But it is also true that Christ's love is there first. He does not wait for us to be reconciled before loving us. He loves us even in the midst of our sinfulness, although we behave as if we are his "enemies", as St Paul put it.

"Indeed, rarely will anyone die for a righteous person – though perhaps for a good person someone might actually dare to die. But God proves his love for us in that while we still were sinners Christ died for us... For if while we were enemies, we were reconciled to God through the death of his Son, much more surely, having been reconciled, will we be saved by his life" (Rom 5:7-8,10).

God's forgiveness in Christ precedes our acknowledgement of our sin. Christ crucified offers his forgiveness to all, and it is this forgiveness which "justifies" us. But if forgiveness is there first, it is, as it were, an offer which awaits our acceptance, once we have acknowledged our guilt. This is why in the Christian tradition confession, repentance and contrition are part of the mystery of our reconciliation as free and responsible beings.

In the same way, victims who forgive their torturers, as Jesus did, are in some way calling them to conversion, and thus to justice, in the hope that they will own the wrong they have done and recognise their guilt for the sake of their own future.

Forgiveness on the part of the victim and the confession of the offender liberate them both from the past.

If those who commit an offence refuse to be converted and accept justice they condemn themselves before God, but it is a matter for their own conscience and no longer concerns their victim.

Above all the victims need to know that their fathers acknowledge the crime they have committed. Unless this happens, no authentic exchange can take place between them. The daughter who, for the sake of her own survival, chooses to make public her father's crime, is at the same time doing him a service. By taking him to court, even against the advice of all around her, she is forcing him to face up to his own actions and his own responsibility.

Eva Thomas,
who was raped by her father at the age of fifteen

Those victims who take the initiative and offer forgiveness can, in contrast, be at peace with their conscience. Some people feel a kind of inner, personal obligation to offer forgiveness without waiting for an explicit gesture of repentance from the offender, but this does not hinder in any way the course of human justice.

The moralist Vladimir Jankélévitch, who has written extensively on the theme of forgiveness, seems to me to be trapped into a certain amount of self-contradiction on this point; he writes that there can be no forgiveness without a confession of wrong-doing but at the same time claims that forgiveness is as gratuitous as love and that the one who forgives must forgive for no reward and with no expectation of a change of attitude in the offender.

Finally it seems clear to me that it is impossible to forgive oneself, for the simple reason that it is only through the eyes of Christ or the eyes of another person that I can know myself to be something more than the wrong with which I am obsessed, the wrong which keeps me trapped within myself. This explains why, in the gospel stories, the fact that Jesus looks at people plays such an important part in their conversion.

9.

Gospel forgiveness, not humanism

How can we experience forgiveness as more than merely excusing or forgetting? How can we prevent it from causing humiliation in another or the breakdown of our relationship with them? How do we forgive without feeling self-righteous? Can we hope to avoid all such pitfalls?

Moralists know all too well that human forgiveness is never entirely pure. The one who forgives may well gain a certain superiority over the offender who will always be in their debt. Victims who forgive generously may well nourish a secret pride in their action. Such feelings would falsify any future relationship between victim and offender.

> *When two people come face to face and one asks forgiveness of the other, God is present. God exists in the words they use, in the moment itself, in the exchange which takes place, in the emotion involved and nowhere else. For what is happening at that moment is of greater importance than any number of angels and than all the trumpets in heaven.*
>
> Ingmar Bergman

When forgiveness is weighted by feelings either of superiority or of bitterness, there is no true reconciliation. In the end we must accept that if we try to understand and explain forgiveness simply on a human level, we will always come up against the impossible or the paradoxical.

For this reason I am inclined to think that forgiveness – meaning forgiveness as manifested and lived out by Jesus Christ – is impossible for human beings in their own strength. Gospel forgiveness implies that a person moves into a new kind of human relationship, governed by the grace of God and the selfless love of Christ.

We should not try to "humanise" the forgiveness we find in the gospel. Society can get by without it. In the end, human beings can survive without forgiveness as they can without faith. Society can function well enough without the forgiveness revealed and bestowed by Christ. By dint of excuses, compensatory actions, the ability to keep silent and forget and at the cost of broken relationships, life somehow goes on... But is this really that "life in all its fullness" which God desires for humanity?

To forgive humanity is a greater task than the creation of heaven and earth.

St Thomas Aquinas

Of all the well-springs of joy, I know of none more abundant, none more inexhaustible than forgiveness.

Cardinal Etchegaray

Now that we have looked briefly at what Christian forgiveness is not, we must try to discover what it really is, its origin and specific conditions.

10.

God's self-revelation –
the basis of biblical forgiveness

Forgiveness springs from the heart of God

In biblical tradition forgiveness is one of the manifestations of the mystery of God who shows himself to be
"full of mercy". The story of the Exodus, the event
which lies at the heart of the liberation and faith of the
people of Israel, is described as an act of mercy. "I have
observed the misery of my people... I have heard their
cry... Indeed I know their sufferings and I have come
down to deliver them" (Ex 3:7-8).

For the people of the covenant, God's mercy is primarily something known by experience. Their history
has taught them that the living God is gracious and
gives his love freely. There are two key words which
are used in the Hebrew Bible to express this graciousness.

The first of these, *hesed*, contains such a wealth of
meaning that it is translated in our bibles by a range of
words which includes love, tenderness, goodness, mercy
and grace. In human relationships it suggests an attitude

of great kindness which goes far deeper than mere mutual good-will. It involves keeping faith with oneself and being faithful to another person – a faithfulness based on true commitment.

When applied to God, the word *hesed* is always used in the context of his covenant with Israel. This covenant is a gift of grace, a manifestation of the graciousness of his love and tenderness.

> *All the paths of the Lord are steadfast love and faithfulness.*
>
> Ps 25:10
>
> *I have not concealed your steadfast love and your faithfulness from the great congregation... let you steadfast love and your faithfulness keep me safe forever.*
>
> Ps 40:10,11
>
> *Steadfast love and faithfulness will meet; righteousness and peace will kiss each other. Faithfulness will spring up from the ground and righteousness will look down from the sky.*
>
> Ps 85:10-11

This idea of mercy involves far more than the forgiveness of sins. It is shown throughout the Bible to the poor, the widow and the orphan whom God loves in a special way, just as a mother will show particular tenderness towards a handicapped child.

God's forgiveness is indeed the expression of his very being. God is consistently faithful to his covenant in spite of the unfaithfulness of Israel, a people which does not always honour its commitment to God. God's love is faithful because he cannot deny himself nor the truth of his being. (In Hebrew, there is one word which can be translated as both faithfulness and truth.)

The close connection between love and faithfulness is expressed by the frequent pairing of the words "grace and faithfulness". Mercy is primarily God's faithfulness to his own nature; his faithfulness to the promise of his Word.

Mercy, God's revelation of his very being

On Sinai, Moses received a first revelation of the very depths of God's being. Although his people have already proved unfaithful, he tells Moses that he, God, is free to bestow his gracious mercy on whom he pleases and that, in the end, his tenderness can overcome sin and evil.

"The Lord passed before him (Moses), and proclaimed 'The Lord, the Lord, a God merciful and gracious, slow to anger, and abounding in steadfast love and faithfulness, keeping steadfast love for the thousandth generation, forgiving iniquity and transgression and sin, yet by no means clearing the guilty, but visiting the iniquity of the parents upon the children and the children's children, to the third and fourth generation'" (Ex 34:6-7).

We may be shocked at this last verse, but it is simply a Semitic way of saying that God allows the consequences of sin to affect even the fourth generation, in order to make clear the seriousness of sin and to demonstrate that our actions have repercussions not only for our own future, but for the future of our children and our children's children. But his loving mercy lasts to the thousandth generation, in other words, for ever.

> *Seek the Lord while he may be found, call upon him while he is near; let the wicked forsake their way, and the unrighteous their thoughts; let them return to the Lord, that he may have mercy on them, and to our God, for he will abundantly pardon.*
>
> *For my thoughts are not your thoughts, nor are your ways my ways, says the Lord. For as the heavens are higher than the earth, so are my ways and my thoughts than your thoughts.*
>
> Is 55:6-9

Burdened by sinfulness and having broken the covenant, Israel had no right to expect God's mercy according to the law. But inspite of her unfaithfulness, the prophets still appeal to Israel not to give up hope; God is faithful to himself, his love is responsible and consistent.

"It is not for your sake, O house of Israel, that I am about to act, but for the sake of my holy name" (Ezek 36:22).

A mother's heart in the heart of God

The other expression used in the Bible to suggest God's mercy is "compassion" – *rahanîm* – which introduces a feminine, maternal element. (It comes from the root *rehem*, meaning the mother's breast.)

The biblical revelation is aimed at helping us to understand that between God and humanity there exists the same kind of bond as that which unites a mother and her child. It is a relationship of unique depth, a special kind of love which is beyond comparison. This love for humanity does not result from any personal merit; it

56

arises out of a compelling need in the very heart of God. It is gracious and tender, full of patience and, with a mother's understanding, always ready to forgive.

"Zion said, 'The Lord has forsaken me, my Lord has forgotten me.' Can a woman forget her nursing child, or show no compassion for the child of her womb? Even these may forget, yet I will not forget you" (Is 49:14-15).

"Is Ephraim my dear son? Is he the child I took delight in? As often as I speak against him, I still remember him. Therefore I am deeply moved for him; I will surely have mercy on him, says the Lord" (Jer 31:20).

Looking ahead to the gospels, we see that when Christ (or those characters in the parables who represent Christ or God the father), is described as being "moved with pity", the phrase used is in fact a translation of this concept of maternal compassion already present in the Old Testament. Christ, then, can truly be called the incarnation, the visible manifestation of the mercy of the God of the covenant.

Thus God loves us with a father's heart, or as a mother whose child is deeply part of her, flesh of her flesh. This maternal or paternal love, a love which is faithful and merciful, will naturally give rise to forgiveness. It will manifest itself as an unceasing longing to return sinful humanity to a "state of grace", to re-establish the covenant broken by human sinfulness, to reconcile humanity through love and to hold out hope for the future and the chance of salvation.

Forgiveness means being restored to a place within the covenant of love

Whether individual or collective, sin, or in other words the breaking of the covenant, is nevertheless an opportu-

The psalmists' cries often give expression to this confidence in God's mercy towards those who do not deceive him and who recognise their sinfulness.

Have mercy on me, O God, according to your steadfast love; according to your abundant mercy blot out my transgressions.

Ps 51:1

Then I acknowledged my sin to you, and I did not hide my iniquity; I said, 'I will confess my transgressions to the Lord', and you forgave the guilt of my sin.

Ps 32:5

But they flattered him with their mouths; they lied to him with their tongues. Their heart was not steadfast toward him; they were not true to his covenant.
Yet he, being compassionate, forgave their iniquity, and did not destroy them; often he restrained his anger, and did not stir up his wrath. He remembered that they were but flesh, a wind that passes and does not come again.

Ps 78:36-39

nity for God to reveal that he is indeed a God of tenderness. This is what gives Moses the courage to go on praying for the sins of his people:

"Moses bowed his head toward the earth, and worshipped. He said, 'If now I have found favour in your sight, O Lord, I pray, let the Lord go with us. Although this is a stiff-necked people, pardon our iniquity and our sin, and take us for your inheritance'" (Ex 34:8-9).

The bible represents the sinner (or sinful humanity in general) as an insolvent debtor whose debt is freely cancelled by God. "Forgive the iniquity of this people according to the greatness of your steadfast love, just as you have pardoned this people, from Egypt even until now" (Num 14:19).

On each occasion, forgiveness is so real and effective that God no longer remembers the sin which he has cast behind him and destroyed. "Surely it was for my welfare that I had great bitterness; but you have held back my life from the pit of destruction, for you have cast all my sins behind your back" (Is 38:17).

There is no human or legal justification for forgiveness. Even the prophets sometimes think that God would be acting justly if he "vented his anger" against the terrible sinfulness of humanity. But in the end they recognise that God's ways are not our ways, and that he does not seek to destroy.

"My people are bent on turning away from me. To the Most High they call, but he does not raise them up at all. How can I give you up, Ephraim? How can I hand you over, O Israel? ... My heart recoils within me; my compassion grows warm and tender. I will not execute my fierce anger; I will not again destroy Ephraim; for I am God and no mortal, the Holy One in your midst, and I will not come in wrath" (Hos 11:7-9).

Far from wanting the death of sinners, God longs for them to repent so that he can have the joy of forgiving and of "re-creating".

"Have I any pleasure in the death of the wicked, says the Lord God, and not rather that they should turn from their ways and live?" (Ez 18:23). Throughout the Old Testament we are shown that "his ways are not our ways".

In biblical history God's mercy, as shown by his unfailing forgiveness, is not simply theoretical. It is a revelation lived and experienced both individually and collectively. Sinful human beings become aware of this mercy when they discover in their lives a love which pursues them, a love which calls them ceaselessly inspite of their wretchedness.

In fact it is often in the very depths of our sinfulness that we are given a glimpse of God's infinite mercy. Our wounds often provide the openings through which God's grace may penetrate.

Bless the Lord, O my soul, and do not forget all his benefits – who forgives all your iniquity, who heals all your diseases, who redeems your life from the Pit, who crowns you with steadfast love and mercy, who satisfies you with good as long as you live so that your youth is renewed like the eagle's.

The Lord is merciful and gracious, slow to anger and abounding in steadfast love. He will no always accuse, nor will he keep his anger forever.

He does not deal with us according to our sins, nor repay us according to our iniquities.

For as the heavens are high above the earth, so great is his steadfast love toward those who fear him; as far as the East is from the West, so far he removes our transgressions from us.

As a father has compassion for his children, so the Lord has compassion for those who fear him.

For he knows how we were made; he remembers that we are dust...

Ps 103:2ff.

The disconcerting fact that God's forgiveness is offered to all can provoke some very differing reactions. Jonah is representative of the whole people of Israel; he refuses to acknowledge God's forgiveness of the inhabitants of Nineveh (Jonah 3:10; 4:2).

In contrast, the Book of Wisdom celebrates a God who loves all that he has made and who has compassion on all. It speaks of a God who longs for people to repent and who thus closes his eyes to their sins. If at times he punishes, he does so in order to teach people the consequences of their wrong-doing.

"But you are merciful to all, for you can do all things, and you overlook people's sins, so that they may repent. For you love all things that exist, and detest none of the things that you have made, for you would not have made anything if you had hated it.

"How would anything have endured if you had not willed it? Or how would anything not called forth by you have been preserved? You spare all things, for they are yours, O Lord, you who love the living.

"For your immortal spirit is in all things. Therefore you correct little by little those who trespass, and you remind and warn them of the things through which they sin, so that they may be freed from wickedness and put their trust in you, O Lord" (Wisdom 11:23–12:2).

11.

God's love is demanding and intends great things for humanity

Although God's tenderness may sometimes be talked of in terms which reduce it to a kind of sweet and insubstantial candy-floss, his mercy is no soft option. A father's love for his child is always exacting simply because he loves that child. God in his love intends great things for humanity.

God knows that the influence of evil can seriously affect our human development and our future and can destroy our human dignity. The Bible talks of the "wrath of God", but this is no more than a way of saying that the consequences of humanity's own wrong-doing have been brought to light. "God's devouring fire" is simply an image for the fire of human sinfulness which devours humanity.

"...no one spared another. They gorged on the right, but still were hungry, and they devoured on the left, but were not satisfied; they devoured the flesh of their own kindred; Manasseh devoured Ephraim, and Ephraim Manasseh, and together they were against Judah. For all this his anger has not turned away; his hand is stretched out still.

> *After the hardship of exile, the psalmists will refer to God as the "God of forgiveness" and the "God of mercy".*
>
> *"But... our ancestors acted presumptuously and stiffened their necks and did not obey your commandments; they refused to obey, and were not mindful of the wonders that you performed among them; but they stiffened their necks and determined to return to their slavery in Egypt. But you are a God ready to forgive, gracious and merciful, slow to anger and abounding in steadfast love, and you did not forsake them."*
>
> Neh 9:16-17

"Ah, you who make iniquitous decrees, who write oppressive statutes, to turn aside the needy from justice and to rob the poor of my people of their right, that widows may be your spoil, and that you may make the orphans your prey! What will you do on the day of punishment...?" (Is 9:19–10:3).

God's mercy can be limited only by the hardening of the human heart. The one sin which God is powerless to forgive is the refusal to be forgiven.

Throughout the Old Testament we are aware of an alternation between unrequited love and faithful love, between the "wrath" of God at the unfaithfulness of humanity, and the mercy and compassion he holds out at once to those who acknowledge their own wretchedness and cry out for his forgiveness.

It is a story of love with moments of great pathos and it is told, by the prophets in particular, in profoundly human terms. God is depicted as losing patience with Israel and deciding to withhold his mercy and punish her. But very quickly he has a change of heart; he is moved with compassion and decides not to give vent to his righteous indignation.

"I will take you for my wife forever; I will take you for my wife in righteousness and in justice, in steadfast love and in mercy" (Hos 2:3).

Even as they warn of the most dreadful catastrophes to come as a result of the rejection of God's love, the prophets never fail to point out that God is always ready to put aside his anger.

"For a brief moment I abandoned you, but with great compassion I will gather you. In overflowing wrath for a moment I hid my face from you, but with everlasting love I will have compassion on you, says the Lord, your Redeemer.

"This is like in the days of Noah to me: just as I swore that the waters of Noah would never again go over the earth, so I have sworn that I will not be angry with you and will not rebuke you.

"For the mountains may depart and the hills be removed, but my steadfast love shall not be removed, says the Lord, who has compassion on you" (Is 54:7-10).

Open shame, O Lord, falls on us, our kings, our officials, and our ancestors, because we have sinned against you. To the Lord our God belong mercy and forgiveness, for we have rebelled against him.

(Dan 9:8-9)

God does not bear grudges. He forgives so that people may have life. His mercy is not to be measured by human standards, for he takes pleasure in giving freely, in forgiving and in ceaselessly re-creating.

"Who is a God like you, pardoning iniquity and passing over the transgression of the remnant of your possessions? He does not retain his anger forever, because he delights in showing clemency.

"He will again have compassion upon us; he will tread our iniquities under foot. You will cast all our sins into the depths of the sea. You will show faithfulness to Jacob and unswerving loyalty to Abraham, as you have sworn to our ancestors from the days of old" (Mic 7:18-20).

This mercy is universal; it is offered to all. For a while the people of Israel believed that, as the chosen nation, they alone were to receive mercy. But no one has an exclusive right to God's merciful love. Those writing after the exile refer increasingly to the universality of God's love. The story of Jonah is in fact a satirical comment on those who would prefer to set their own narrow limits on God's tenderness:

"The compassion of human beings is for their neighbours, but the compassion of the Lord is for every living thing" (Sir 18:13).

God's mercy – a lesson taught over centuries

If God is merciful, he expects those whom he has created to show the same mercy towards one another. But mercy does not come naturally to human beings and more often than not they turn against each other. Throughout the Bible we see how the revelation is also a long process of education for human beings, patiently teaching them "to be merciful even as their heavenly father is merciful".

66

> *There is hope for your future, says the Lord: your children shall come back to their own country.*
>
> *Indeed I heard Ephraim pleading: "You disciplined me, and I took the discipline; I was like a calf untrained. Bring me back, let me come back, for you are the Lord my God.*
>
> *For after I had turned away I repented; and after I was discovered, I struck my thigh; I was ashamed, and I was dismayed because I bore the disgrace of my youth.*
>
> *Is Ephraim my dear son? Is he the child I delight in? As often as I speak against him, I still remember him. Therefore I am deeply moved for him; I will surely have mercy on him, says the Lord.*
>
> Jer 31:17-20

God desires mercy and mutual love more than all acts of worship, all gifts, sacrifices and burnt offerings. This is something which is laid down when the covenant is first formulated:

"You shall not wrong or oppress a resident alien, for you were aliens in the land of Egypt. You shall not abuse any widow or orphan... If you lend money to my people, to the poor among you, you shall not deal with them as a creditor; you shall not exact interest from them. If you take your neighbour's cloak in pawn, you shall restore it before the sun goes down; for it may be your neighbour's only clothing to use as cover; in what else shall that person sleep? And if your neighbour cries out to me, I will listen, for I an compassionate... You shall not delay to make offerings from the fullness of your harvest and from the outflow of your presses" (Ex 22:21ff).

The kind of fasting which is truly pleasing to God is that which arouses in us an attitude of mercy towards others

67

"Is not this the fast that I choose: to loose the bonds of injustice, to undo the thongs of the yoke, to let the oppressed to free, and to break every yoke? Is it not to share your bread with the hungry, and bring the homeless poor into your house; when you see the naked, to cover them, and not to hide yourself from your own kin?" (Is 58:6-7).

For I desire steadfast love and not sacrifice.

Hos 6:6

Already a connection has been established between justice and tenderness. "He has told you, O mortal, what is good; and what does the Lord require of you but to do justice, and to love kindness and to walk humbly with your God?" (Mic 6:8).

But it will be many years before the concept of solidarity extends beyond the limits of race and religious belief. Following the prompting of God's spirit, the prophets will at length open Israel's heart to the fullness of God's love. "For I am God and no mortal" (Hos 11:9).

It will require centuries for the lesson in mercy to be learnt, for human beings find it so hard to leave a wrong unavenged and to feel no bitterness. It is only with the last of the Wisdom books that we finally begin to trace the outlines of the message of Jesus: that forgiveness is offered to all.

"The vengeful will face the Lord's vengeance, for he keeps a strict account of their sins. Forgive your neighbour the wrong he has done, and then your sins will be pardoned when you pray. Does anyone harbour anger against another, and expect healing from the Lord? If one has no mercy toward another like himself, can he then seek pardon for his own sins? If a mere mortal harbours wrath, who will make an atoning sacrifice for his sins? Remember the end of your life, and set enmity aside; remember corruption and death, and be true to the commandments. Remember the commandments, and do not be angry with your neighbour; remember the covenant of the Most High, and overlook faults" (Sir 28:1-7).

12.

Jesus Christ,
God's forgiveness made incarnate

"Whoever has seen me has seen the Father" (Jn 14:9). If what Jesus says is true, then we must believe that in him we have been given a totally new revelation of God's mercy and of his forgiveness in particular.

For at the beginning of the New Testament John the Baptist, "the foremost of the prophets", is still threatening those who do not repent with "the wrath to come" and the "unquenchable fire" (Mt 3:7,12).

Even Jesus' disciples found it hard to set aside this radical view of things. They are ready to "command fire to come down from heaven" on those who refuse to receive him (Lk 9:54).

The idea that purification can be achieved by brute force will be challenged by the disconcerting attitudes of their "Master". Not only does Jesus welcome sinners and eat with them, he announces that he has come not to condemn sinful humanity, but to heal and forgive.

"Those who are well have no need of a physician, but those who are sick." Jesus takes as his own the words which the prophet Hosea had already ascribed to the

God of the covenant : "Go and learn what this means, `I desire mercy, not sacrifice.' For I have come to call not the righteous but sinners" (Mt 9:13)

This is why the good news proclaimed by Jesus is indeed something utterly new. He did indeed come to set fire to the earth; not the fire of God's wrath or vengeance, but of his merciful love.

"Indeed, God did not send the Son into the world to condemn the world but in order that the world might be saved through him" (Jn 3:17).

The one who takes away a consciousness of sin and replaces it with a consciousness of forgiveness is taking away a heavy burden and replacing it by a light burden... "Faith says: forget everything but remember forgiveness."

Kierkegaard

Jesus' whole life is the ultimate and astounding revelation of God's mercy, a God who is full of concern for humanity and deeply affected by human misery. As in the gospel stories of the Canaanite woman, the father of the epileptic boy, the two blind beggars of Jericho, he is a God to whom one can call out with confidence, "Lord, have mercy."

He is the Good Samaritan, "moved with pity" for the man who was left wounded at the road side. Not only does he not reject sinners and those who are "unclean", he goes so far as to touch them and invites himself to their homes: "Zacchaeus, hurry and come down; for I must stay at your house today... For the Son of Man came to seek out and save the lost" (Lk 19:1-10).

72

The mystery of the cross – love without measure

Christ is the incarnation of God's forgiveness. He reveals the infinite depths of this forgiveness on the cross: "Father, forgive them; for they do not know what they are doing" (Lk 23:34). "To believe in the crucified Son means 'to see the Father' in this act which reveals the secret depths of his heart", writes the Pope in his encyclical *Rich in mercy*.

Such is the measureless extent of God's forgiveness which sets free the human heart and gives humanity the power to forgive the unforgivable. "This is my blood of the covenant, which is poured out for many for the forgiveness of sins" (Mt 26:28). Divine love alone could achieve this level of forgiveness and so become the source of new life for those who are victims as well as for those who murder. Christ shows us the seriousness of our sin and, at the same time, the depth of God's love and forgiveness.

The "God who is rich in mercy" (Eph 2:4) is the one whom Jesus Christ reveals to us as Father. It is the Son who has shown us the Father and made him known to us in himself.

John Paul II, *Rich in mercy*

In granting forgiveness, Jesus did not close his eyes to the horrors of evil nor did he forget the tragedy of sin but he took upon himself all its consequences. Even in glory, his body will bear the scars eternally.

Christ is the "first-born" of salvation, the first-fruits of a new creation. Of him God can say; "My son who was dead is alive again."

Forgiveness freely granted

Because of the limitations of the human condition, the path of forgiveness is fraught with dangers and snares. Probably the only way to avoid them is to have experienced personally the graciousness of Christ's forgiveness.

Can anyone who has not been forgiven truly forgive as Christ asks us to forgive? Forgiven not simply for one particular sin, but from a fundamental state of sinfulness. For if sin is a matter of wounding, spoiling, rejecting and losing love, then all our wrong-doings are ultimately wrongs directed against God who is Love.

No amount of penitence can make amends for an offence against Love. Thus God's forgiveness is a gift of grace. In the same way, if my wrong-doing has been against my neighbour's love, what action can make up for the hurt I have done them?

Forgiveness is necessarily always a mystery of grace, yet it does not reduce us to a humiliating state of childish dependence. The forgiveness which flows from unconditional love is an invitation to live and grow and love as He does.

In the Judeo-Christian revelation there is a close connection between God's mercy, the forgiveness of sins, peace and salvation. Forgiveness is one of the most powerful manifestations of the salvation which God has desired for humanity since the beginning of history. At the dawn of Christianity, the Virgin Mary and Zechariah each proclaims this forgiveness; "His mercy (hesed) is for those who fear him from generation to generation... He has helped his servant Israel, in remembrance of his mercy" (Lk 1:50,54).

13.

Forgiveness brings healing and makes possible a new future

Not only does Jesus proclaim God's forgiveness, he proves by his actions that he has the power to forgive, a power which belongs to God alone.

"When he returned to Capernaum after some days, it was reported that he was at home. So many gathered around that there was no longer room for them, not even in front of the door; and he was speaking the word to them. Then some people came, bringing to him a paralysed man, carried by four of them. And when they could not bring him to Jesus because of the crowd, they removed the roof above him; and after having dug through it, they let down the mat on which the paralytic lay. When Jesus saw their faith, he said to the paralytic, 'Son, your sins are forgiven.' Now some of the scribes were sitting there, questioning in their hearts, 'Why does this fellow speak in this way? It is blasphemy! Who can forgive sins but God alone?' At once Jesus perceived in his spirit that they were discussing these questions among themselves; and he said to them, 'Why do you raise such questions in your hearts? Which is easier, to say to the paralytic, Your sins are forgiven, or to say, Stand up and take your mat and walk? But so that you may know that the Son of Man has authority on earth to forgive sins' – he said to the paralytic – 'I say to you, stand up, take your mat and go to your home.' And he stood up, and immediately took the mat and went out before all of them; so that they were all amazed and glorified God saying, 'We have never seen anything like this!'" (Mk 2:1-12).

It is the faith of a community of believers which brings the paralysed man to Jesus who in turn responds by saying not "I forgive you" but "Your sins are forgiven". His words point back to the Father, the one who is at the source of all forgiveness. In the same way, on the cross, Jesus does not say "I forgive them" but "Father, forgive them."

Forgiveness means liberation, deliverance, re-creation. The need for forgiveness can never be overstated. It restores a sense of joy and liberty to those who are weighed down by their guilt.

Forgiveness implies neither that a wrong has been forgotten nor that it has been condoned. It is an expression of our willingness to trust in our neighbour.

Jean Delumeau

Jesus responds in a way which goes far beyond our immediate expectations. There are different kinds of paralysis affecting not only the body, but also the mind, the heart and the soul. Thus Jesus first addresses the need for liberation at the deepest level of being. Physical healing will then be simply a sign of the more radical healing which God alone can effect. In offering forgiveness Jesus is deliberately revealing his divine identity.

Since the right to forgive belongs exclusively to the God of the covenant, Jesus' promise that "Your sins are forgiven" is greeted as a scandal and creates uproar.

In the eyes of the scribes who witness the event, Jesus has blasphemed by making himself God's equal. It is a matter of serious consequence.

Jesus' attitude arouses either amazement or praise. He poses a question which must be answered today as then. Who is this man who does what God alone can do? This is the question at the heart of our faith. To believe in forgiveness means to accept God's sudden and unpredictable involvement in the very heart of our suffering world, a world so often closed against him by sin. To believe in forgiveness is to believe that a new world can be established in the person of Christ.

Forgiveness makes possible a new future

"I say to you, stand up." In this scene we are already witnessing the Paschal Christ who came to restore humanity. Through him God gives us grace and raises us to new life. Forgiveness is always an act of hope, a rebirth to a new future for humanity. To forgive is to say to someone who is paralysed by their past: "Stand up and walk."

Forgiveness does not imply a refusal to face the realities of human existence; it means making the choice to look with hopefulness, just as Jesus looked at Mary Magdalen, Zaccheus or Peter. This does not demand the kind of pious blindness which sees everyone as "good" and "nice", but a refusal to identify human beings with the evil which they do.

Jesus never condones evil – he knows it for what it is and fights against it even to the death – but his goal is the victory of life. Only the spirit of Christ dwelling within us can enable us to look beyond the murderer's face, believing that obscured within it we will find another face, radiant with light, a reflection of the creator God.

Faith alone can go on hoping that the wrong-doer, too, will one day discover the presence of this image of God which nothing can completely destroy, and that they will come to respect that image both in themselves and in others.

Jorgè Valls who was a prisoner for twenty years in Cuba maintains that for him "forgiveness was the foundation stone on which to build the future once out of that hell. And that stone must be placed without knowing what the other person will do with it. To forgive is to give utterly, to go to the very extreme of generosity."

To forgive is not to deny that evil and suffering have been caused and experienced. It does not mean that the past is forgotten or wiped away; the risen Christ still bore the marks of the cross. Forgiveness is not an attempt to put right the past, it is a preparation for the future. Forgiveness is no side issue, it is a full participation in creation and resurrection.

Xavier de Chalendar

Forgiveness is an act of creation

What could be more creative and liberating than the granting of forgiveness. When we forgive we are saying to someone: "You exist", "You are worth more than your wrong-doing, more than your crime." It demands great confidence in humanity and a great faith in the future to be able to break free from the vicious circle of guilt and vengeance.

The words "faith" and "confidence" come from the same Latin root. To have confidence means to believe in progress, to trust that it is always possible for people to change. One of the greatest dangers in human relationships is to keep others imprisoned in their past.

Human beings are, by nature, "incomplete". As they grow, they continue to discover their own identity and to reveal that identity to others. But such growth and progress are only possible through contact with others who believe in them and trust them. This is true not only of school children, but also of adults in their daily work or in their relationships. It is trust which gives love its power.

As human beings we are continually being born, gradually emerging as if from a chrysalis of clay through the life-giving warmth of love. There are often people waiting to be loved before they become better, while we are waiting for them to become better before we love them.

Love is the deep-lying power through which we come to know our true identity and all that makes us who we are. Both those who forgive and those who are forgiven witness to the fact that human greatness lies in the rediscovery of human dignity.

We do not offer forgiveness simply because otherwise life would be unliveable. Forgiveness arises from a growing awareness of a mysterious, inner prompting of the Spirit of God whose "greatest glory is in the life of humanity". And what is life other than the promise of a future, the possibility of action and the potential for growth and fruition in spite of temporary sterility?

In God's eyes there is a future for every person, as long as they believe in it, and as long as those around them encourage them to go on believing, in spite of the wrong they have suffered. "The opposite of sin is faith", as Kierkegaard said.

The only possible way of moving forward is along the path of forgiveness which alone can bring true liberation and a fresh start. But if this is to happen, one of those involved, and in most cases the victim, must have the "incredible" idea – though it cannot occur in the human heart without the prompting of grace – of being the one who begins to love the first and who offers their love to someone who feels no love in return.

There is nothing "reasonable" about this. As we have said, forgiveness belongs to the realm of grace. "Where sin abounds, grace abounds in greater measure", wrote St Paul. When Adam marred his relationship with his creator through sin, it was God who made the first move: "Adam, where are you?"

"Blessed are the merciful." Blessed are those who are able to forgive. Jesus regards forgiveness as a blessing, since through forgiveness we are able to share in some way in the very being of God. By offering forgiveness, we "resemble" him a little more. In a very real way we create something new and bring into being something totally unexpected.

"If you love those who love you... do not the pagans do as much?" Do something new, says Jesus, be as inventive as your Father in heaven. Be merciful. Be creative!

14.

The parable of the merciful Father
(Lk 15:11-32)

As we have seen, it is impossible fully to understand sin, forgiveness and Christian reconciliation without going back to the sources of the revelation in which mercy is shown to be an essential element in the very being of God.

One of the best known parables through which Jesus reveals God's infinite and creative tenderness, the roots of sin and the source of all reconciliation, is the story of the prodigal son, or rather, to convey the real thrust of the teaching, the story of the merciful father.

The father is the central character in the story and his two sons feature simply as a means of bringing his attitudes to light. There is often a temptation to read the gospels merely to find a set of rules telling us what to do and what not to do, while forgetting that, first and foremost, Jesus' purpose is the revelation of who God is and what he does for us.

Before we explore the parable itself it is worth seeing what can be learnt from its context. "Now all the tax collectors and sinners were coming near to listen to him.

And the Pharisees and the scribes were grumbling and saying, 'This fellow welcomes sinners and eats with them.' So he told them this parable..." (Lk 15:1-3).

Jesus' extraordinary behaviour has challenged the moral and religious codes of the scribes and Pharisees and this parable comes in response to their scandalised murmurings. They, like us, are unable to comprehend the measurelessness of God's love as revealed in Jesus' actions. Theirs is still a religion of duty, law and merit. So Luke sets this "parable of revelation" in a dramatic context: that of humanity, unable to receive the grace of God's love.

In the three so-called "parables of mercy" – the stories of the lost coin, the lost sheep and the prodigal son – Jesus is trying to convey that the motivation behind his behaviour has its roots deep within the very mystery of God and his covenant.

The parable is a literary masterpiece in its own right. It comprises two parallel scenes, unequal in length, with a departure from, and a return to, the father's house. The house is at the centre of the narrative and is symbolic of a number of things. It may suggest the community of the people of the covenant, the Church, the kingdom of God, and thus the intimacy of the life of the Trinity itself.

'This son of mine was dead and is alive again!' (Lk 15:4-24)

The story opens with the younger son who can be seen as a symbol for the people of God, but also for the heathen, the sinner or of humanity as a whole in its alienation from God.

His departure is described in terms of the breaking

off of a relationship. Jesus is wanting to convey to us the perennial drama of human sinfulness. In the face of the father's freely given love, the prodigal son wants to make a life of his own. We are reminded of Adam, who, in the garden of paradise, wanted to eat the fruit of the tree of the knowledge of good and evil, rejecting the distinction between them and thus, too, creating his own set of values. The roots of sin lie in this demand for absolute autonomy. Human sinfulness is essentially the breakdown of the relationship between child and father. Human beings, created by God's love, are unaware, through ignorance, pride or ingratitude, of their own mystery.

The desire for self-sufficiency leads to self destruction. The Evil One makes quite clear what he is offering: "You will be like God" (Gen 3:5). Human beings are always trying to be in absolute control, to put themselves in place of God.

In order to remain faithful to his own nature, the father concentrates on the human dignity of his lost son... the father is aware that what is essential has been saved; his son's humanity. Although that son has wasted his inheritance, his humanity is still intact.

John Paul II, *Rich in mercy*

Human beings have not understood that it is the Father's love which is the source of their being, their identity, their life, growth, purpose and happiness. They have not grasped that God's love does not deny their freedom, but is in fact fundamental to their very being.

This is the journey made by the prodigal son who

longs to take charge of his own life, to have control of all the wealth which he thinks belongs to him by right. "Give me the share of the property that will belong to me." He has not understood that all he is and all he has is a free gift of his father.

Of course, like all the parables, this story can be read on many different levels. The young man could well be seen as a symbol for the people of the covenant who have so often tried to take for themselves the inheritance of the Promised Land, symbolic of the graciousness of God's giving. Jesus' opponents, the Pharisees and scribes at whom this parable is addressed, are a clear illustration of such and attitude.

"So he divided his property." God takes the huge risk of creating humans as free beings, thus courting eventual rejection. Love cannot impose constraints without denying itself. Love does not impose itself, it offers itself, gives itself, suggests, invites.

"The younger son... travelled to a distant country." The fact that the son leaves home is not in itself serious. Every child who is to grow into a responsible adult must, sooner or later, become independent to some extent. "Leaving the family fold" does not imply breaking away from the "family home". The child can become an adult and still stay in a close relationship with its father, whose home will always remain theirs.

The telling point in this case is the fact that the son leaves with the clear intention of breaking off all ties with his father. He presumes that he can find his own identity without the bond of love which unites him to the father. He is shutting out Life and closing in on himself. It is the perennial story of humanity, society and all systems of thought which turn in on themselves and shut out the possibility of transcendence.

"He travelled to a distant country, and there he squandered his property in dissolute living." Sin is a kind of current carrying all before it to a land of waste and destruction. Sinners are those who waste their wealth, their talents, their capacity for love.

"When he had spent everything, a severe famine took place throughout that country, and he began to be in need." When a person has come to the end of their resources: intelligence, talents, capacity for love... they become aware of a great emptiness within them. Jesus here shows himself an able psychologist. Sinfulness is always the land of hunger, drought, boredom and disgust.

When disappointed, unfulfilled and bitter, people may well feel as if they are grasping at shadows. They have the taste of ashes and death in their mouth.

"He went and hired himself out to one of the citizens of that country, who sent him out into his fields to feed the pigs." Being sent to look after pigs is certainly a great humiliation. We should bear in mind that the pig was a sacred animal used in sacrifices to pagan gods and that this was one of the reasons why the Jews would never eat pork. The job of looking after pigs was thus considered to be unclean and shameful.

Some critics see this as a subtle allusion to the wretchedness of the people of Israel in exile, contaminated by their contacts with the pagan world.

"When he came to himself he said..." The first step towards conversion is an acknowledgement of the hopelessness of one's situation.

A feeling of dissatisfaction with the way things are and a thirst for change create an opportunity for seeing things as they really are. A humble acknowledgement that things are going nowhere, a desire to move forward and a belief that change is possible are unquestionably the first elements in any conversion.

"How many of my father's hired hands have bread enough and to spare, but here I am dying of hunger! I will get up and go to my father." The young prodigal does not remain in the grips of morbid, sterile guilt. He has no illusions about himself, unlike those who set themselves up on a pedestal and then bewail the image of their own greatness when their dreams are shattered. Such people are sorry "for themselves". Their guilt is bound up with hurt pride and they remain trapped within themselves.

As for the young prodigal, he, in contrast, stands on his feet – an attitude basic to every incident of conversion in the gospel. "He went to his father."

Even so, what motivates his return is rather ambiguous. We can of course see his decision as being the result of a genuine growth in self awareness: "I am a fool! I had everything I needed in my father's house. I was surrounded by his love and generosity. I have ruined everything! I will return to my father's house; I will regain my integrity, my dignity, my identity as a human being and a son."

However, his decision appears rather more prosaic: "How many of my father's hired hands have bread enough and to spare, but here I am dying of hunger! I will get up and go to my father!" It seems that he is tormented rather more by his empty stomach than by remorse at having rejected his father's love!

"I will say to him, 'Father, I have sinned against heaven and before you; I am no longer worthy to be called your son: treat me like one of your hired hands!" Even if he were to be treated as a servant he would at least be guaranteed his board and lodging. The fine speech he prepares is simply a way of getting out of the awkward situation.

> *The one who receives mercy feels no humiliation, but instead feels as if he has been "found" and given a new sense of value. The father's delight indicates that something important has remained intact: a son, even one such as this, never really ceases to be his father's child.*
>
> John Paul II, *Rich in mercy*

There are critics who think that in keeping with the spirit of this parable, we should not be too eager to turn this prodigal son into a model of conversion. To do so would be to risk once again missing the real thrust of Jesus' teaching.

For if the father had welcomed back with open arms a contrite son, the Pharisees would have had no reason to be scandalised. Israel had long known that God welcomed back repentant sinners. If Jesus had insisted, as they did themselves, on the usual procedures of expiation and penitence his opponents would have had no quarrel with him. What they question is Jesus' quite different attitude which resembles that of the father in the story.

Jesus does not wait to see whether the sinners he meets show signs of genuine contrition. He invites himself into their homes. In the same way, only one thing seems important to the father in the parable: the fact that his son has returned. It matters very little that his motives are not entirely pure.

In fact, as we have said already, Jesus does not place his emphasis on the behaviour of the son, but rather on the freely given love of the father and on the joy he feels in giving and forgiving.

"While he was still far off" – far from life and from love, and lost in the far country of his sin – "his father saw him and was filled with compassion." (Literally the expression used is "bowels of compassion", the same phrase that is used of the God of the covenant.)

God loves us enough to wait for us daily along the road of our life's journey. His patient love is always there ahead of us. Moved with compassion, he always takes the initiative in meeting us and offering forgiveness. He it is who first comes out from his house to meet the sinner. "He ran and put his arms around him and kissed him."

The reference to him coming out of the house could well be a subtle allusion to the mystery of the incarnation, to the coming of Jesus to this earth to be alongside sinful human beings.

The father's reaction reveals much about the kind of relationship God desires to have with sinful humanity. He does not seek to humiliate. Thus, as in the majority of conversion scenes in the gospel (cf the way Jesus simply looks at Mary Magdalen) there is no lengthy moralising, no complicated examinations of conscience.

"He put his arms around him and kissed him." God knows that his child is hurt. He is aware of the bitterness of all that his child has just experienced. He knows that that child needs tenderness far more than words to heal his wounds and restore his will to live.

"Quickly, bring out a robe – the best one – and put it on him; put a ring on his finger and sandals on his feet." The word "quickly" conveys the impatience of God's love, his longing to restore sinful human beings to their status as his children. In the Bible, clothing is traditionally a symbol for restored integrity.

The ring, which often bore the family seal, was a symbol of power in noble or royal families. Pharaoh, for example, takes off his ring and puts it on Joseph's finger, thus giving him authority over all his wealth (Gen 41:42). Sandals, too, are a sign of a freedom.

The prodigal regains all his privileges as a son of the household and is once again free to make use of his father's property. The feast which follows is yet another sign of his restoration, since the son can once again take his place at the family table with his father. Some people even see this as a subtle allusion to the eucharistic meal, the feast for forgiven sinners.

The parable is an illustration of a perennial situation: it is the story of every human being, for all of us have wandered far from our true homes. Our lives are a long journey back to the father's house, the house of love. This is the very heart of the revelation which enlightens the mystery of our relationship with God.

15.

Forgiveness –
a licence for lawlessness?

The scandal of forgiveness (Lk 15:25-32)

Let us now look at the second part of the parable. It is
written to parallel the story of the younger son, but is
less developed. "Now his elder son was in the field; and
when he came and approached the house..."

Once again, there is a return to the father's house.
When the elder son discovered what was going on, "he
became angry and refused to go in. His father came out
and began to plead with him." Again, it is the father
who comes out of the house to meet his son.

> *Be tolerant with one another and forgiving, if any of you*
> *has cause for complaint, you must forgive as the Lord*
> *forgave you.*
>
> Col 3:13

However, the elder son refuses to go into his father's
house, and replies: "Listen! For all these years I have

91

been working like a slave for you, and I have never disobeyed your command; yet you have never given me even a young goat so that I might celebrate with my friends".

"Working like a slave", "disobeyed your command"... the choice of vocabulary fools no one! Such words are always in the mouths of the scribes and Pharisees who could hardly fail to recognise themselves in this elder son, scandalised by the father's attitude just as they themselves are scandalised by Jesus' behaviour.

Like the elder son, they think that they have acquired certain rights. What is the good of making such efforts to fulfil the demands of the law if the very first sinner who comes along has a right to the same consideration? It's just not fair! This man Jesus is undermining the very foundations of religion and morality.

I remember the reaction of a mother whose son had just run away. In the course of a conversation which centred around this parable, she said with great annoyance: "But it's a licence for bad behaviour!"

Through the words of the elder son, Jesus clearly exposes his opponents' attitude. He certainly understands them and, according to their own logic, they are not wrong! But Jesus longs to lead them on towards a new way of thinking which transcends human logic: the way of God's measureless love.

Finally, the elder son clearly shows that he has not yet grasped the true extent of the covenant based on grace and unconditional love. He does not know his father's heart. What is more, he never once uses the word "father". He speaks like a hired servant.

With great skill, Luke creates a contrast between the vocabulary used by the elder son and that used by his father: "But when this son of yours came back..." He distances himself from his brother. (A little like when a father, exasperated by his children's naughtiness, blames his wife for the bad behaviour of "her" children.)

The father replies "Son, you are always with me, and all that is mine is yours... this brother of yours was dead and has come to life."

The elder son must take his part in the mystery of the covenant, he must receive the father's spirit of mercy, he must set aside his "slave mentality" and learn to see himself as a son who is freely loved. Only when he has rediscovered his own identity as a son in the light of the father's tenderness can he recognise himself as his brother's brother.

Jesus is careful not to provide a conclusion for his story. He leaves it to each listener to make their own decision. He does not seek to pass judgement, even on the scribes and the Pharisees. Rather, he invites each person to find a new, individual motivation: the measureless mercy of God.

In the romance languages, the word "forgiveness" which comes from the Latin perdonare, *meaning to give utterly, to cancel a debt completely, is not originally a theological term, but a literary one. It appears for the first time in a Latin translation of one of Aesop's fables, and comes up again in the language of the troubadours:* "amarai donc en perdos", *thus I love for nothing, freely, in vain.*

Alain Gouhier

This is a God who shows himself to be neither paternalistic nor the supreme upholder of order, but one who offers an invitation to the freedom of love. What is of greatest importance is neither the Law nor patriarchal order, but the quality of the relationship between God and humanity.

The self-abasement of God, who in Jesus Christ left his throne of glory in order to come among us, is the first act of forgiveness. Without imposing constraints and without denying our humanity, he stands beside us to forgive us.

Forgiveness implies, on the part of the one who offers it, the strength to resist making it an instrument of domination. Human beings are too weak to be able to forgive the wrongs inflicted by another without any trace of superiority. God alone, precisely because he is all-powerful and all-loving, can limit his own power, can choose powerlessness and thus grant true forgiveness without humiliating. It is the work of grace.

Christian forgiveness is not some kind of general amnesty decreed from on high by a powerful ruler. It is our point of contact with the living God who makes himself our equal. He does not reject human beings, even though they have offended him by turning aside from his gift of love. What greater offence can there be to love than scorn?

Such is gospel forgiveness, the gift of the spirit, which frees human beings from the need to dominate, thus enabling them to forgive and to ask for forgiveness without condemning them to a permanent feeling of indebtedness. This kind of forgiveness alone can open up a way towards new and creative relationships.

16.

Confession brings growth not humiliation

When I was ten years old I stole some money from my mother's purse which she always left in a drawer in the kitchen ready to pay the traders who frequently passed by. It was a childish crime with no serious consequences.

Yet I had a strange feeling that my relationship with my mother had somehow changed and that she no longer looked at me in the same way. This upset me a great deal. The idea that she loved me less than before became unbearable.

One question alone filled my mind: how was I to regain my mother's love? For her part she never made any comment and never reproached me. But her silence weighed on me. I would much rather she had got angry with me, shouted at me, even hit me. But she did nothing, and this silence ate away at me. One evening I decided to break through the barrier of silence which imprisoned me.

My mother was busy cooking the evening meal. I hung around her feeling awkward and miserable, not knowing how to bring up the subject. Then I suddenly blurted out: "Mummy, I stole some money from your purse." My throat felt tight. My mother hardly flinched. She glanced at me quickly and, carrying on with what she was doing, said no more than "Oh."

Then silence. It was awful. I had to break it, fill it, get rid of it. Since she still said nothing, I burst into tears and almost shouted at her: "Do you still love me?"

In that instant everything changed. My mother left her cooking, ran to me, took me in her arms and kissed me: "Don't be silly, of course I still love you! You're my little boy! We'll say no more about it."

I could tell my mother was even more upset than I was. In just a few moments her love had been regained and had wiped away all my misery. I felt forgiven and was so grateful. And in fact she never did speak of the incident again.

I have included this childhood memory because, for me, it helps shed light on the mystery of God's forgiveness. I had discovered that to confess a crime to someone who loves you, is to experience a sense of liberation rather than humiliation. How many Christians imagine that they have to approach God in a certain way, disguising their wretchedness under their "Sunday best", so as to appear worthy. They are tragically mistaken about God's love if they seek to be worthy of it!

God's love is vulnerable, just like a mother's love. "His heart is moved within him" when one of his children comes to him in torment and confesses their wretchedness. A little boy who has hurt himself does not hide his injury from his mother. He knows by instinct that by showing her he will awaken her maternal tenderness.

When the prodigal son returns, his father asks him no questions about his past. God never desires to humiliate those whom he has created.

Does our own mother remember all our childhood aches and pains? When we were learning to walk and stand, how often we knocked into tables and side-boards! How many times did we end up with gashed lips or cut eyes? We may perhaps bear the scars on our knees even now! But once we have reached adulthood and have taken responsibility for our own lives, our mother can look back and laugh at the memory of our growth towards freedom.

I believe that God is more interested in our future and in our spiritual growth than in our past. He always looks forward, never behind.

I truly believe that to confess one's fault before the love of God is not an act of surrender, but one that brings growth and liberty. It is strange that today people will often confess more readily to their psychiatrist who charges them hundreds of pounds, than to their Father, whose forgiveness and love are there for the asking!

I am always amazed and astonished when someone comes to me to make their confession without trying to justify themselves or make any subtle excuses, but simply calling a spade a spade, a sin a sin. That person grows in my estimation. It is a fine thing when a person acknowledges their limitations! And I am not God.

17.

How often should we forgive?

"Then Peter came and said to him, 'Lord, if another member of the church sins against me, how often should I forgive? As many as seven times?' Jesus said to him, 'Not seven times, but, I tell you, seventy-seven times'" (Mt 18:21-22).

Peter knows full well that he must forgive; but how often? When he suggests seven times he imagines that he is being generous and acting in the spirit of Jesus. It is after all a commendable attempt when we think that the rabbis, after careful study of the scriptures, taught that one should forgive up to three times!

It seems strange that Jesus should reply using language which echoes the vengeance and violence of the song of Lamech: "If Cain is avenged sevenfold, truly Lamech seventy-seven fold" (Gen 4:24). But he transforms this vicious spiral of violence into a limitless spring of forgiveness.

He demonstrates that within the new community which is inaugurated in his person, forgiveness knows no measure. If this is to happen, each individual must accept their status as an "insolvent debtor", whom God freely forgives and welcomes into his kingdom. Jesus goes on to illustrate this relationship between God and sinner in a parable.

> *As God's chosen ones, holy and beloved, clothe your-selves with compassion, kindness, humility, meekness, and patience. Bear with one another and, if anyone has a complaint against another, forgive each other; just as the Lord has forgiven you, so you also must forgive.*
>
> Col 3:12-14

All of us are insolvent debtors

"For this reason the kingdom of God may be compared to a king..." A man who owes the huge sum of sixty million pounds is brought before him. At the mention of such a far-fetched amount, we know that this is no true story but an illustration of our true situation before God: that of insolvent debtors.

According to the experts, the king's cruel decision to have the man sold along with his wife, his children and all his possessions, has no precedent in Jewish legal practice but is instead reminiscent of the customs of some pagan countries. This feature of the parable is primarily aimed at emphasising the desperate nature of the man's situation, thus creating an element of surprise when the debt is suddenly cancelled.

There is in fact no way out of the situation according to the law. But those listening to the parable are invited to base their thinking on an alternative premise. The king grants his servant more than he asked. His initiative is spontaneous and unexpected, and things can suddenly move forward.

The feeling which motivates this king is once again expressed in terms of the divine "compassion" of the covenant God. The story indicates that by forgiving us, God gives up all ideas of retribution and any possibility of exacting justice.

There is no act of penitence, no amount of suffering and no kind of punishment which could correspond to our sinfulness. God longs for "insolvent" humanity to be fully restored. No amount of punishment could bring this about!

However, in this story, the servant has hardly been let off before he is ready to attack one of his fellow servants and demand from him the payment of a petty amount of money. This other servant pleads for time, and, significantly, uses the same words which the first servant had earlier addressed to the king.

But the one who had been let off his debt had his fellow servant thrown into prison. This is not a feature of Jewish law either. Being put in prison for debt was a pagan practice which must have appeared particularly inhuman to those who were listening to the parable.

> Be kind to one another, tender-hearted, forgiving one another, as God in Christ has forgiven you. Therefore be imitators of God, as beloved children, and live in love, as Christ loved us and gave himself up for us, a fragrant offering and sacrifice to God.
>
> Eph 4:32–5:2

The narrative places great emphasis on the contrast between the two situations. In the end, the king becomes the dread judge at the end of the age. "I forgave you all that debt because you pleaded with me." The seriousness of the servant's fault lies in the fact that he did not show the same compassion to his fellow servant as his master had shown to him. Jesus concludes by saying:

"So my heavenly Father will also do to every one of you, if you do not forgive your brother or sister from your heart" (Mt 18:35).

Our experience of the Father's merciful love as revealed in Jesus must become a source of forgiveness within us. The conclusion of this parable is at the same time the final word of Matthew's teaching on community. The Church of Christ is not founded on the power that coerces, but on mutual forgiveness.

The Church is the steward of divine forgiveness. We are responsible together for the liberating forgiveness of the Father. From now on each one of us is judged on the way we accept and share with others the forgiveness we receive from the Father.

Little children, let us love, not in word or speech, but in truth and action. And by this we will know that we are from the truth and will reassure our hearts before him whenever our hearts condemn us; for God is greater than our hearts, and he knows everything.

Jn 3:18-20

"Forgive us... as we forgive"

"Forgive us our trespasses as we forgive those who trespass against us."

How many Christians have a problem with this demand in the Lord's Prayer? Are we to think that our own attitude is a condition of God's forgiveness, as if we were asking God to imitate our own generosity?

Human beings can never dictate to God. Thankfully,

God does not need us to take the initiative before he loves and forgives us. In creation as in the history of salvation, all is given, all is grace. However generous our response, it will never fully compare with God's loving initiative.

> *Whenever you stand praying, forgive, if you have anything against anyone; so that your Father in heaven may also forgive you your trespasses.*
>
> Mk 11:25

Besides, we will never be able to make up completely for all the opportunities for loving which we have missed and all the hurt we have caused in our relationships with God and with others, or even for the wrongs we have brought on ourselves through our refusal to love.

The verse does in fact begin by an appeal for that gracious forgiveness which is to "convert" the way we live out all our relationships. "Forgive us."

The words which follow, "as we forgive those who trespass against us" are aimed at Christians who have already experienced God's forgiveness in their lives and who thus want to show that they now live according to this "grace".

We are no longer talking in terms of rights and merit; it is rather as if we are putting ourselves on the same wave length as God. The requirement found in the Lord's Prayer is in fact an appeal for conversion. It is asking us to be in harmony, in tune with his love. By forgiving those who have sinned against us we will show that we too have become a part of the circle of freely offered love.

If I refuse to forgive my neighbour, I am obstructing
the outpouring of God's love and forgiveness. I am
preventing the power of love from spreading and growing in the world through my actions. I am hindering the
flow of universal love which alone can save the world.

This is why Matthew ends the Lord's Prayer with the
words: "For if you forgive others their trespasses, your
heavenly Father will also forgive you; but if you do not
forgive others, neither will your Father forgive your
trespasses" (Mt 6:14-15).

Lastly, and most importantly, we should never forget
that when we say this prayer we are praying with Christ.
For the Our Father is the prayer of the Son before it is
ours. He alone could say "forgive us as we forgive". It is
in communion with him, through the power of his Spirit,
that we can address the Father in this way. We are in
fact asking him to bring about in our lives that which
Jesus lived out in his Passion.

"Be merciful, just as your Father is merciful" (Lk 6:36)

Throughout the history of the revelation, the people of God have gradually amended their idea of mutual forgiveness according to their experience of God's forgiveness.

So, paradoxical as it may appear, the famous *lex talionis* was proof of a positive evolution in comparison with what was being practised in contemporary civilisations, since it set a limit to the scale of vengeance permitted. "An eye for an eye and a tooth for a tooth." But no more than that!

But by his own behaviour and teaching on forgiveness, Jesus reveals something totally new about God's mercy which shakes the very foundations of the way human relationships are lived out and which transcends all our notions of forgiveness.

So while chastening us you scourge our enemies... so that, when we judge, we may meditate upon your goodness, and when we are judged, we may expect mercy.

Wis 12:22; see also 19-21

"You have heard that is was said, 'You shall love your neighbour and hate your enemy.' But I say to you, Love your enemies and pray for those who persecute you, so that you may be children of your Father in heaven; for he makes his sun rise on the evil and on the good, and sends rain on the righteous and unrighteous. For if you love those who love you, what reward do you have? Do not even the tax collectors do the same? And if you greet only your brothers and sisters, what more are you doing than others? Do not even the Gentiles do the same? Be perfect, therefore, as your heavenly Father is perfect" (Mt 5:38-48).

Here we are suddenly confronted with God's measureless generosity. We are being invited into a kind of relationship which no longer fits within our human logic; the logic of God's love obeys a very different set of rules. It is an "unreasonable" love!

Jesus does not hesitate to give us as a model his Father and ours. He invites us to take God as the pattern for our human relationships and thus for the way we should live out forgiveness. "Be perfect as your heavenly Father is perfect!" In other words: "Love as God loves."

"Blessed are the merciful, for they will receive mercy" (Mt 5:7). Christian forgiveness is a blessing, a key to happiness, a way into the kingdom of God. Christians are continually invited to follow their Master's example and, like him, overcome evil with good: "Do not be overcome by evil, but overcome evil with good" (Rom 12:21).

Those who are disciples of Christ can be recognised by their ability to forgive, as the deacon Stephen, the first Christian martyr showed by forgiving his enemies as he died (Acts 7:60).

18.

Forgiveness – a gift of the Spirit of the risen Christ

"When it was evening on that day, the first day of the week, and the doors of the house where the disciples had met were locked for fear of the Jews, Jesus came and stood among them and said, 'Peace be with you.' After he said this, he showed them his hands and his side. Then the disciples rejoiced when they saw the Lord. Jesus said to them again, 'Peace be with you. As the Father has sent me, so I send you.' When he had said this, he breathed on them and said to them, 'Receive the Holy Spirit. If you forgive the sins of any, they are forgiven them; if you retain the sins of any, they are retained'" (Jn 20:19-23).

The disciples are utterly dejected, torn between feelings of bitterness and a desire for vengeance after the death of the one they knew to be righteous. It is Christ's risen presence and the power of his Spirit which break open their hearts and liberates them from their fear.

After his resurrection, Jesus' first encounters with those who had "betrayed" him involve gestures of forgiveness. Thus at the lake-side he asks three times of

Peter, who had denied him three times when he was arrested: "Peter, do you love me?" So Peter is tactfully and kindly restored by the grace of forgiveness.

> *The days are surely coming, says the Lord, when I will make a new covenant with the house of Israel and the house of Judah... I will put my law within them, and I will write it on their hearts; and I will be their God, and they shall be my people. No longer shall they teach one another, or say to each other, "Know the Lord", for they shall all know me, from the least to the greatest, says the Lord; for I will forgive them their iniquity, and remember their sin no more.*
>
> Jer 31:31-34

Jesus "unlocks" the disciples' hearts and converts their memories. He shows them the marks of his passion which they must not forget. They must own the pain and suffering which has been, without becoming trapped in the past. Through Jesus a new future is made possible.

The remission of sins, the ability to forgive and to be forgiven is a gift of the crucified and risen Christ, won by his victory over evil and one of the signs of the birth of a new humanity.

What we are talking about here goes beyond the "sacrament of reconciliation" passed on by the apostles to their successors. Every human being, through the power of the Spirit, is now able to forgive freely.

Forgiveness and messianic peace

Forgiveness is intrinsic to the salvation promised by the God of the covenant and to messianic peace. Peace be with you! It is not by chance that the gift of forgiveness is linked to that of peace. There can be no peace without forgiveness.

No one can go through life with a heart full of bitterness. Hatred imprisons the memory, paralysing the individual and destroying both their inner peace and their relationships with others. Those who do not forgive, however serious the wrong they have suffered, will never be at peace.

Thus from the first Easter, the gift of forgiveness is a fundamental element of salvation, of the restoration of liberated human beings and of the re-birth of a new humanity.

Forgiveness has been made possible, but it is still an essentially free act. It remains difficult, just as freedom itself is difficult. A person can refuse to forgive. Yet from now on human greatness lies in the ability, through the power of the spirit of Christ who overcame sin and death, to offer this gesture of paschal forgiveness – a gesture which will always involve death and re-birth. It is an act of liberation and creation for both offender and victim.

From now on, in the light of the living Christ whose love was stronger than cowardice, betrayal, torture and death, there is no crime which can not be forgiven.

I will take you from the nations, and gather you from all the countries, and bring you into your own land. I will sprinkle clean water upon you, and you shall be clean from all your uncleanness, and from all your idols I will cleanse you. A new heart I will give you, and a new spirit I will put within you; and I will remove from your body the heart of stone and give you a heart of flesh. I will put my spirit within you, and make you follow my statutes and be careful to observe my ordinances. Then you shall live in the land that I gave to your ancestors; and you shall be my people, and I will be your God. I will save you from all your uncleannesses.

Ezek 36:24-30

Forgiveness, fruit of the reconciliation between God and humanity

Once again it is in the light of the events of Easter that we can understand more fully how forgiveness must not be confused with reconciliation. Within the biblical revelation, the themes of the covenant, of salvation, reconciliation, peace and forgiveness are closely interwoven and often shed light on each other, yet they each remain distinct.

Forgiveness is one of the fruits of a wider reality which, in Christianity, is called "the mystery of salvation" and which St Paul talks of in terms of "reconciliation".

I may be able to forgive someone who has wronged me, but I have no power to reconcile that person with God. The risen Christ alone has the power not only to forgive all people freely, but also to reconcile them with God, drawing them back into the covenant and into intimacy with God.

The people of God had gradually gone deeper into the mystery of reconciliation through their painful experience of the permanent gulf between God's call and their own inability to live according to the demands of the covenant. The forms of worship laid down by Moses contained many rites of expiation and purification for a whole range of sins. All of these rites were, in the end, designed to bring about an impossible reconciliation between God and humanity.

The prophets realised that rites such as these could never achieve any real reconciliation, so deep is the divide between God and humanity. Human beings are wounded in their very being, scarred by the sin of refusal. God alone could change people's hearts and bring about a complete reconciliation. If the roots are diseased, it is useless to prune the tree; its fruit will still be diseased. The roots themselves must be dealt with.

In the incarnation, God does indeed take the initiative once again, inaugurating a new covenant which the prophets had seen as a radical purification, a reconciliation of the human heart at its very depths.

"Christ is our peace and our reconciliation"

The words of the risen Christ on Easter morning are proof that this perfect and definitive reconciliation has now been accomplished. It is a reconciliation which affects not only the people of Israel, but humanity as a whole. It is a reconciliation which goes beyond human boundaries, to be a source of universal peace.

"But now in Christ Jesus you who were once far off have been brought near by the blood of Christ. For he is our peace; in his flesh he has made both groups into one and has broken down the dividing wall, that is, the hostility between us... that he might create in himself one new humanity in place of the two, thus making peace, and might reconcile both groups to God in one body through the cross, thus putting to death that hostility through it.

"So he came and proclaimed peace to you who were far off and peace to those who were near; for through him both of us have access in one Spirit to the Father" (Eph 2:13ff).

19.

Living out reconciliation

"Be reconciled to God"

Forgiveness involves a new birth. When God forgives us in Jesus, he creates a truly new being.

"So if anyone is in Christ, there is a new creation: everything old has passed away; see, everything has become new! All this is from God, who reconciled us to himself through Christ, and has given us the ministry of reconciliation; that is, in Christ God was reconciling the world to himself, not counting their trespasses against them, and entrusting the message of reconciliation to us. So we are ambassadors for Christ, since God is making his appeal through us; we entreat you on behalf of Christ, be reconciled to God. For our sake he made him to be sin who knew no sin, so that in him we might become the righteousness of God. As we work together with him, we urge you also not to accept the grace of God in vain" (2 Cor 5:17–6:1).

This freely given reconciliation does not result from some purely external edict; it is not simply a piece of legal make-believe, it is an ontological fact. It involves nothing less than a "new creation", achieved by the death and resurrection of Christ. What was once impossible for humanity has become possible. But it is still up to us to open ourselves to this act of creation.

> *For in him all the fullness of God was pleased to dwell, and through him God was pleased to reconcile to himself all things, whether on earth or in heaven, by making peace through the blood of his cross. And you who were once estranged in mind, doing evil deeds, he has now reconciled in his fleshly body through death, so as to present you holy and blameless and irreproachable before him.*
>
> Col 1:19ff

For although God has taken the initiative in this reconciliation, he longs for our collaboration in this spiritual adventure. Reconciliation is both a gift of God and, at the same time, a commitment on the part of humanity.

At the heart of the Church's mission is the proclamation of this Good News, the "Gospel of reconciliation", in which forgiveness plays a key role. It is a message of universal reconciliation between God and humanity, between human beings, and between humanity and the rest of creation.

Every Christian is now, as St Paul puts it, an "ambassador" for Christ who gives us a "new heart" indwelt by his Spirit, enabling us to live out his forgiveness in every area of our lives, both personal and collective.

In the Synod in 1983, bishops from around the world spent time in reflection on the Church's "mission of reconciliation". All Christians were invited to discern the places where Christ is calling us, today, to live out the mission of reconciliation.

We cannot undertake such a mission without looking closely at the causes of division in our own daily lives and analysing what lies behind the conflicts in our streets and cities and throughout our country.

Our first task is therefore to become aware of the divisions which are currently tearing apart the human family on a local and international level, and to discern where the Spirit is calling us to be creators of universal reconciliation in Jesus Christ. Forgiveness is a daily undertaking; it is ceaselessly at work, renewing the fragile fabric of our human relationships, continually restoring to wholeness broken relationships between couples, families and society.

There is a need for reflection and comment geared to each individual area in which we must live out this kind of forgiveness; such a task however is beyond the scope of this present book.

In particular, we should ask ourselves if Christ's forgiveness is relevant in, for example, political life. Can one party forgive another? It is after all most often on the collective level that the utopian ideal of gospel forgiveness seems the least practical and even impossible.

Certainly any kind of simplistic "other-worldliness" is to be avoided since this tends to idealise reality while disregarding the fact that a group is something more than the sum total of its individual members. And yet, unless we are to relegate the Good News to the land of make-believe, Christians must have the courage to become involved in social conflicts while trying to live out the reconciliation offered by Christ.

Finally, in connection with what has already been said on the subject of forgiveness and memory, it is perhaps up to Christians to demonstrate how forgiveness, which brings with it hope for the future inspite of the wounds of the past, is an act which also "converts" the collective memory.

The trials of certain war criminals attract a huge amount of publicity because they raise a question as to what actually constitutes a "crime against humanity". The collective memory is very much alive, its past wounds still unhealed.

How can society free itself from such painful memories? How can it avoid being determined today by what happened in the past and yet, at the same time, not forget? In these areas of life, the Christian must be open to the light of the risen Christ which alone can bring about reconciliation.

20.

The sacrament of paschal growth

Finally, it would not be right to conclude this all too brief survey of the problem of forgiveness without a mention of the sacrament of reconciliation and the difficulties which appear to stand in the way of its rehabilitation today. We must of course bear in mind that one particular attitude towards confession in which it is seen more as a way of wiping out sins than an opportunity for the restoration and growth of human dignity, has resulted in the creation of guilt rather than liberation.

At one time people talked of the "chapter of faults". Today, the expression "sacrament of reconciliation" is preferred as being more in keeping with the gospels.

Indeed, most of the gospel stories of conversion and forgiveness take place in an atmosphere of joy which often culminates in the sharing of a celebratory meal. There is the shepherd's joy at finding his lost sheep; the joy of the housewife who finds her lost coin; the joy of the prodigal's father at his son's return to life; the paschal joy of the banquet of resurrection life at God's table.

We have already discussed how the parable of the prodigal son is in fact an illustration of the way each one of us travels through life as on a long road, leading back to the Father's house, towards the love which is freely given in the kingdom of God. The story can also be seen as an illustration of the journey made by Jesus himself who became one with us in our sinfulness and who, on Easter morning, "returned" to the Father's house, "came back" to life... He is indeed the "first-born son", the heir who makes each of us co-heirs with him of the Father's inheritance.

God is life, and those who distance themselves from God risk death. The Father's creative love is a kind of sacrament; it brings us back to life, delivers us from our sin through new birth and renews in us our delight in life.

The stories of the prodigal son, of Mary Magdalen and Zacchaeus, for example, all show how the movement towards conversion and "sacramental reconciliation" should never be seen as a kind of narcissistic introspection, but rather as a way of de-centering oneself, of moving the focus away from one's own wretchedness, and turning (which is the etymological meaning of the word conversion) towards God.

To encounter Christ in this sacrament involves our acceptance through faith of a word of life which recreates us, cleanses us and gives us peace: "Go, your sins are forgiven you! Go, your faith has saved and freed you. Go in peace..."

"Go", "Get up", "Walk": these are the key words found in the gospel stories of forgiveness. We are to stand up in order to move forward anew; herein lies a way to the rediscovery of the true meaning of Christian confession.

In the gospel stories, forgiven sinners are never presented as stiff and formal; they are full of life, leaping

118

with joy at the discovery that they are loved once again and that they have value in God's eyes in spite of their sinfulness.

Through Jesus we are shown that God's pleasure lies in creating us and in seeing us fully alive. The sacrament of reconciliation is a sacrament of journeying, a sacrament of "paschal growth" for each of us who are gradually discovering our identity as children and co-heirs, and, in the light of Christ, continually opening ourselves to our individual truth as human beings.

Living out our baptismal life

Thus whenever we make an act of confession it should be seen in the context of the fullness of our baptismal life. In baptism we received as it were the seeds of new life, a life as children and co-heirs; but a whole life-time is needed for these seeds to germinate and grow to maturity.

This "sacrament of growth" is a work of the Spirit of Christ who patiently shapes the "new being" which is there in embryo in each one of us. "God invents us afresh each day out of what we are." God's love is a kind of energy, a creative power which transforms us gradually, always respectful of our fragile liberty.

Through God's love we are forgiven and, in spite of our weakness, that love gives us the joy of moving beyond our limitations. Paradoxical as it may seem, I have often noticed that those who are unable to see themselves as they really are, feel self-hatred far more readily than self-love. And those who have no more love for themselves, who no longer feel any sense of wonder at the dignity which God has given them, are no longer able to love others.

> *The scribes and the Pharisees brought a woman who had been caught in adultery; and making her stand before all of them, they said to him, "Teacher, this woman was caught in the very act of committing adultery. Now in the law Moses commanded us to stone such women. Now what do you say?" They said this to test him, so that they might have some charge to bring against him. Jesus bent down and wrote with his finger on the ground. When they kept on questioning him, he straightened up and said to them, "Let anyone among you who is without sin be the first to throw a stone at her." And once again he bent down and wrote on the ground. When they heard it, they went away, one by one, beginning with the elders; and Jesus was left alone with the woman standing before him. Jesus straightened up and said to her, "Woman, where are they? Has no one condemned you?" She said, "No one, sir". And Jesus said, "Neither do I condemn you. Go your way, and from now on do not sin again."*
>
> Jn 8:1-11

Making one's confession does not imply feeling bitter about who one is; that would merely be demoralising. Even the idea of looking into oneself still implies a kind of "self-centredness". In the gospels, conversion involves a movement in exactly the opposite direction. To be converted means to stand up, to leave oneself behind and go towards one who waits for us; towards Jesus, the "sacrament" of the Father's forgiveness.

Neither conversion nor forgiveness are possible without a degree of trust and the belief that I am loved with the ceaseless love of Christ: "I have come to seek out and save that which was lost." Conversion suggests a personal experience of God's love. It can never arise from a set of moral rules and regulations but only from an encounter with the One who makes me aware that I am loved, called to live and to become a free person.

We must be careful not to confuse Judas' remorse with Peter's repentance. Judas withdrew into himself and was trapped there. He was so appalled by the knowledge of his own wretchedness that he destroyed himself.

Peter was just as much a sinner, and he, too, denied his master. But he had felt Jesus looking at him: "The Lord turned and looked at Peter" (Lk 22:61). The look in Jesus' eyes, free of all hatred and full of tenderness, overwhelmed him, drew him out of himself and put an end to any thoughts of suicide.

Through the expression in Jesus' eyes he felt called to free himself from his desperate situation. It was as if Jesus were saying to him: "My poor Peter, look what a mess you have got yourself into again. Come, don't stay here feeling wretched and miserable. And when you have returned, strengthen your brothers."

In the light of Christ's life and through his words and gestures, we are made aware of the shadows and darkness in our own lives, and of our refusal to love. He alone can give us the courage to act in truth without despairing of ourselves, because we know that he loves us. There is no humiliation in the recognition of one's own wretchedness before God; through his love our confession brings freedom and nobility.

Educationalists are well aware that if a child is starved of affection, its development will be seriously affected. The same applies in spiritual life. Love is vital to the soul's health. In Christianity, God himself puts on the servant's apron and washes the feet of those whom he has made.

There are so many people who are left with feelings of self-hatred, convinced that they are too wretched for God to care about them. But God does not love us because we are in any way "worthy". Rather, it is his love which makes us "loveable" and gives us our dignity.

It is often said that twentieth century human beings no longer have any sense of sin. I am more inclined to believe that they have lost all sense of God's love.

Only followers of Christ who have personally experienced God's forgiveness, can themselves attempt to live out this forgiveness in their relationships with others and, with a realistic faith, try to live through the inevitable family disputes and social conflicts, in the presence of the Father of all mercy.

Michel Hubaut

LISTENING TO SILENCE

Silence, it would seem, is not much appreciated in
today's world. Or it is held to be a luxury, though it is
one we cannot do without, psychologically, spiritually,
even physically. It is good to break away sometimes
from the din, the tension and the rush of modern society
and find peace and tranquillity in contemplating in
silence. It is the purpose of this book to provide paths to
this peace. The desert and solitude are the keynotes of
the book but 'Paths of Silence' shows the value of
silence above all in the life of contemplative prayer in
the heart. It is in praise of silence, not in psychological
reference only but as leading to holy silence in the
presence of God. There are two paths to silence, one
solitude, the other, paradoxically, relationships, knowing when to be silent and when not. We need to find
again the way to the heart by means of knowledge of
God and of human beings through spiritual understanding and a new way of loving. Twofold also are the
results of silence in outgoing to God and to others.
Then, too, there is God's silence. Why does he not
intervene?

This is not a theological treatise. It is intended only
to help a person to faith.

Michel Hubaut, Franciscan, is a writer and facilitator,
experienced in giving conferences and retreats.

ISBN 085439 478 8   pages 92

John Arnold

THE QUALITY OF MERCY
A fresh look at the Sacrament of Reconciliation

"The sacraments are such vital gifts for the life of the
Church and we must be prepared to question and de-
velop our own understanding of them. This is particularly true in the Sacrament of Reconciliation. Whilst
the years since Vatican II have seen developments in
our theological understanding of this sacrament, I sus-
pect that not enough has been said about how we should
set about using it well or to consider why so many
people apparently no longer choose to use it at all.

This book offers a guide and helps to ask the questions that we should all be addressing about our personal use of the sacrament. It reminds us of the first and
most important element of God's love for us and the
expression of that love through forgiveness and en-
couragement.

Westminster Cathedral has a long tradition in providing for the celebration of the Sacrament of Reconciliation. It is appropriate that this book comes from a
chaplain at the Cathedral and I welcome the invitation
that it makes to reflect on the importance that this
sacrament can have for each one of us.

I recommend this book to you in the hope that it will
instil a new sense of gratitude for that quality of mercy
which is not strained."

Basil Hume OSB
Cardinal Archbishop of Westminster

085439 433 8   128pp